WAITING
FOR
JESUS

WAITING FOR JESUS

An Advent Invitation to Prayer and Renewal

RICH VILLODAS

WATERBROOK

WaterBrook

An imprint of the Penguin Random House Christian Publishing Group,
a division of Penguin Random House LLC

1745 Broadway, New York, NY 10019

waterbrookmultnomah.com
penguinrandomhouse.com

CONTENTS

CONTENTS

PART FOUR: **BEHOLDING**

WAITING FOR JESUS

INTRODUCTION

Christ came.

Christ comes.

Christ will come again.

This summarizes the season of Advent.

For many people, time is oriented around a cultural calendar that we organize life around. Every month, there's a holiday, various school breaks, and rhythms that we keep. But for the person who wants to live into the story of Jesus, a new vision of time is needed.

For the Christ follower, the new year doesn't begin when January 1 arrives; it begins with the news that God came. And that he comes. And that he will come again.

In the church calendar, Advent marks the beginning of the year. It's the start of a new year for the Christian. It reminds us that fresh starts and new beginnings are not products of our willpower, or realities that surface when a new calendar year begins, but rather expressions of God's grace in Christ.

Advent means "arrival." This season compels us to look for the one who arrived on earth two thousand years ago and still arrives in our world today. Advent is preparation for Christ's arrival. It's what Christmas is all about: God with us.

Yet preparing for Christmas is often not focused on Christ. We tend to get ready for Christmas by setting up the Christmas tree, filling stockings, and waiting for the arrival of our Amazon purchases. (Preaching to myself here.) We are culturally formed to prepare more for the arrival of Santa than the coming of Jesus. We leave out cookies and milk by the fireplace (or maybe on the fire escape!).

But setting out cookies and milk is not what preparing for Christ's arrival looks like; rather, we should be preparing our hearts and our attentiveness. The season of Advent opens us up to the surprising ways of God. In Advent, we are invited to wrestle with our longings, desires, and hopes for a world marked by grace, goodness, and peace. It is a time to recall the biblical truth that the renewal of our lives and our world is found in God's coming among us in Jesus Christ. Advent is a season to reignite a spirit of prayer.

Every season in the church calendar has a particular emphasis.

Lent reminds us to place God's ways—and not our appetites—as the guiding principles for our lives. Eastertide calls us to feast and rejoice in Christ's resurrection. Pentecost invites us to be filled with God's life because the Spirit has been poured out. Ordinary time forms us to see God in the mundane.

Advent trains us in hopeful waiting.

In this devotional, you will find twenty-five days of reflections and guided structures for prayer. There are four main sections. Traditionally, the four weeks of Advent are built around the words *hope, peace, joy,* and *love,* but this devotional is based on the words *waiting, peacemaking, rejoicing,* and *beholding.*

My hope is that you will find truth and encouragement to cultivate a life of communion with God in this Advent season—that you would be moved to prayer. My hope is that, by his grace, this book will ground you in the midst of a distracted world, help you wait on Jesus, and discern the ways he arrives in your life today.

To wait well is part of the Christian life. Yet this is what I know to be true about my life and yours: In this season, we might not wait well. We might become impatient and disgruntled and lose hope. But, dear friend, the good news of Advent is not that we are faithful in our waiting; it's that God is faithful in his coming.

HOW TO USE THIS DEVOTIONAL

This book is designed to help you travel through the first twenty-five days of December, culminating in a final reflection meant to be read on Christmas Day. I encourage you to set aside a consistent time and place to read, journal, and pray through this book. I've attempted to make each day's reading brief enough to fit into fifteen minutes; however, those who desire to linger longer may do so.

Each day is comprised of two parts: (1) a devotional written by me that unpacks a portion of Scripture related to one of the four themes of this book (waiting, peacemaking, rejoicing, and beholding), and (2) space to reflect on the day's theme. In the second part, you'll find the following elements to help you enjoy God's presence and go deeper:

- **Prepare:** an invitation to spend a few moments in silence before God

- **Prayer for Presence:** a short prayer to dedicate your time to God

- **Scripture:** a passage to look up in your Bible if you desire to

- **Guide:** a thought-provoking quote from a wise voice in recent or ancient church history

- **Question:** a prompt based on the day's theme that you can pray, discuss, or journal about

- **Closing Prayer:** a way to conclude your
  time and invite God into your day

Depending on how you like to process with God, you may want to have a pen and a notebook or journal nearby. If you're using this devotional with your spouse, family, or small group, the questions might tee up meaningful conversations.

As you embark on this journey through Advent, may the Lord bless you and keep you.

PART ONE

WAITING

THE FOUNDATION OF THE SPIRITUAL LIFE

"Waiting patiently in expectation is the foundation of the spiritual life."[1] These are words from the French writer Simone Weil. I must confess, I don't like these words one bit.

Waiting, for me, is not enjoyable. I'm a native New Yorker, so to hear that waiting is the foundation of the spiritual life unnerves me—and maybe you too.

But there's no getting around it. Our waiting patiently is God's laboratory for our transformation, and I've had to learn that the hard way.

There have been too many Christmas seasons when I'm frantically running up and down the mall on December 23 trying to pick up an item I should have purchased a few weeks before. Turns out I'm not the only one. During a recent holiday season, I took a trip to a New York mall, only to find out that all of Queens had the same idea. I had to wait to get into the parking lot. Wait to find a spot. Wait to get into the store. After amazingly finding my item, I stood in line to make the purchase. Then I repeated the process because I had three more stores to ransack.

At no point in my Christmas-shopping experience did I see people singing Christmas songs while waiting in line. People were angry, frustrated, and irritable. It was a mess. Some people (like myself) did all we could to avoid waiting, but I learned a spiritual lesson while at the mall: Everyone has to wait.

We do all we can to avoid waiting, but no matter what we do to circumvent or avoid it, at some point in our lives, we will have to wait. And God wants to use waiting to transform us.

There's a story in the Gospels about a married couple, Zechariah and Elizabeth, who had to wait to have a baby (see Luke 1). When Luke, the gospel writer, described them, he went all out to highlight their obedience:

> In the time of Herod king of Judea there was a
> priest named Zechariah, who belonged to the
> priestly division of Abijah; his wife Elizabeth
> was also a descendant of Aaron. Both of them
> were righteous in the sight of God, observing all
> the Lord's commands and decrees blamelessly.
> (verses 5–6)

DAY

1

It's noteworthy that Luke mentioned their religious power and lineage. A first-century Jew would probably think that because of how righteous they were, Zechariah and Elizabeth would have a great number of kids. In their culture, it was assumed that the size of your family reflected God's favor. If you didn't have kids, it was interpreted as a sign of his disapproval.

That's why the next sentence in Luke's account would have stunned his readers:

> They were childless because Elizabeth was not
> able to conceive, and they were both very old.
> (verse 7)

DAY

1

How could this righteous couple be childless? Zechariah's name means "whom the Lord remembers," but, sadly, it feels more like God has forgotten them entirely.

At some point, Zechariah is chosen to perform temple duties on one of the most holy days, in the most holy part of the temple. It's a once-in-a-lifetime experience. When the day comes, as he's praying, an angel named Gabriel appears and tells him God has heard his prayer. He will have a son (John the Baptist), who will prepare the way for the Messiah. This news is incredible. At their age, it's truly a miracle.

But what I find particularly astonishing is their attitude toward God even in the painful waiting. They could have turned bitter and resentful. Instead, they held on to him in prayer. They did not get what they desperately desired and *still* remained faithful.

I'm sure their waiting was not perfect. And, dear friend, your waiting will not be perfect either. Even in the valley, it's possible to stay connected to God while allowing yourself to feel all the feels. (Just read the book of Psalms.)

That is the essence of prayer.

Prayer is not about staying connected to God because of what he will give us; it is about remaining connected to him even when we don't get what we want. Like he did for Zechariah and Elizabeth, God *may* bless you with what you've been longing for. But even if he doesn't, his affection is set upon you, and none of your waiting is wasted.

DAY

1

REFLECT

PREPARE: Spend two minutes in silence and stillness before God.

PRAYER FOR PRESENCE: Lord Jesus, in this moment, I believe you want to speak to me in a deep and personal way. May I be attentive to your loving and merciful voice.

SCRIPTURE | LUKE 1:5–25

GUIDE: A waiting person is a patient person. The word "patience" means the willingness to stay where we are and live the situation out to the full in the belief that something hidden there will manifest itself to us. Impatient people are always expecting the real thing to happen somewhere else and therefore want to go elsewhere. The moment is empty. But patient people dare to stay where they are. Patient living means to live actively in the present and wait there. Waiting, then, is not passive. It involves nurturing the moment, as a mother nurtures the child that is growing in her womb.[2]

—HENRI NOUWEN

QUESTION: Which part of Zechariah and Elizabeth's story do you identify with in this season? Have you been waiting on the Lord for something but it feels like he isn't listening? Or, on the flip side, have you seen God provide in a miraculous way? Spend a few minutes reflecting, praying, or writing what you sense God is speaking to your heart.

CLOSING PRAYER: May the Lord bless us and keep us and cause his face to shine upon us from this day forth and forevermore. Amen.[3]

DAY
1

GOD WORKS IN THE DARK

When I think of the difficulty of waiting, the great poet Langston Hughes comes to mind. In his famous poem "Tired," he wrote,

I am so tired of waiting,
Aren't you,
For the world to become good
And beautiful and kind?
Let us take a knife
And cut the world in two—
And see what worms are eating
At the rind.[1]

Yes, Langston, I'm tired too.

I'm tired of the wars.
I'm tired of the division.
I'm tired of the injustices.
I'm tired of the violence.

Advent shouts out, "God is coming!" but sometimes it's hard to see that when we're surrounded by darkness. We are all waiting for something. And sometimes it feels like we're waiting in the dark.

That is where Advent begins. Every year, we come to this season and are reminded that darkness is a reality and that we need God to break through with his light. Darkness, for most of us, is not a good thing, but we have hope, because God works in the dark. In fact, some of the greatest moments in the Bible happened in dark places:

DAY
2

- When God called Jonah, the man ran the other way. His disobedience pulled him into the darkness of a fish's belly. And in that darkness, God revealed himself to Jonah. God works in the dark.

- The prophet Jeremiah was depressed, contemplated suicide, and experienced great darkness. He wrote the book of Lamentations, and in his writing, God revealed his mercy and faithfulness to him. God works in the dark.

- Elijah the prophet was afraid for his life, and while it was night, God visited him in a still small voice. God works in the dark.

- Job lost everything, and through that experience, God met him in great power. God works in the dark.

- When the Israelites were in bondage, God led them out of Egypt by night. God works in the dark.

- The resurrection of Jesus happened "while it was still dark" (John 20:1). God most certainly does his best work in the dark.

The Advent season doesn't promise that if you come to Christ, all your problems will go away. Not at all. Instead, the promise is that even when life seemingly spirals out of control, there is hope.

To wait in the dark can be disorienting and vulnerable. Barbara Brown Taylor once wrote, "Human beings do not lose control of their lives. What we lose is the illusion that we were ever in control of our lives in the first place."[2]

Waiting certainly reminds us that we are not in control.

Maybe that has become painfully true for you. You might be waiting through a period of illness. Or a season of unemployment. Or deep loneliness.

In all that, take heart, dear friend. The darkness need not be a sign that the end is near. In fact, Advent tells us that a new beginning is right around the corner.

REFLECT

PREPARE: Spend two minutes in silence and stillness before God.

PRAYER FOR PRESENCE: Lord Jesus, in this moment, I believe you want to speak to me in a deep and personal way. May I be attentive to your loving and merciful voice.

DAY
2

———— SCRIPTURE | PSALM 27:7–14 ————

GUIDE: Our lives are formed in the hands of a great mystery that does not ask us for our advice.

So if waiting is an aggravation, it is at least partly because we do not like being reminded of our limits. We like *doing*—earning, buying, selling, building, planting, driving, baking—making things *happen,* whereas waiting is essentially a matter of *being*—stopping, sitting, listening, looking, breathing, wondering, praying. It can feel pretty helpless to wait for someone or something that is not here yet and that will or will not arrive in its own good time, which is not the same thing as *our* own good time.

And yet waiting is an essential part of the Christian life. Listen to what we say every time we break bread together: "Christ has died. Christ is risen. Christ will come again." This is the mystery of our faith, that we are always waiting for Christ to come to us even though we believe that he has already come and that he is coming to us right now in word and sacrament.[3]

—Barbara Brown Taylor

QUESTION: What is one area of your life that you struggle to release to God? What would it look like to surrender it to him? Spend a few minutes reflecting, praying, or writing what you sense God is speaking to your heart.

CLOSING PRAYER: May the Lord bless us and keep us and cause his face to shine upon us from this day forth and forevermore. Amen.

REFUSING TO ACT BEFORE GOD ACTS

Moses was nowhere to be found. Forty days earlier, he'd climbed a mountain to be with God, but after waiting for so long, the people of God were restless. *What's taking so long?* Perhaps Moses lost cellphone reception. Or maybe he fell. After all, he wasn't a young man anymore.

As tension mounted, the anxious crowd cornered Moses's brother, Aaron, who had been left in charge. "We're tired of waiting. *Do* something," they said. "It seems like Yahweh has abandoned us. We need someone to guide us."

You probably know what happened next. Aaron gave in, instructing the people to hand over their gold rings—the same rings meant for furnishing the tabernacle, where God wanted to dwell with his people. Aaron melted the rings down, then fashioned them into a golden calf. Despite God's direct warnings *not* to do so, they worshipped the idol they had made (see Exodus 32).

If we rewind this scene, just a few days earlier, God gave them a command, saying, "You shall not make any graven image" (see 20:4). But anxiety will cause you to do some irrational things.

What's the lesson? It's hard to wait upon God when he seems absent or delayed. One of the primary expressions of anxiety is reactivity. It's tempting to take matters into our own hands. Impatience wins over trust, and the results can be disastrous.

This Advent season, let's remember the importance of waiting. Though we can't always see him, God is indeed at work in our lives. In the waiting, he does some of his deepest work inside us.

To wait on God is not a passive act; it's actually a means of positioning ourselves to receive from him in a moment of difficulty. Eugene Peterson wrote, "Waiting in prayer is a disciplined refusal to act before God acts."[1] And God acts within us as we wait on him.

In the book of Isaiah, we find words that don't seem to make sense:

> He gives power to the faint,
>   and to him who has no might
>   he increases strength.
> Even youths shall faint and be weary,
>   and young men shall fall exhausted;

DAY
3

but they who wait for the LORD shall renew
>   their strength;
>   they shall mount up with wings like eagles;
> they shall run and not be weary;
>   they shall walk and not faint.
>   (40:29–31, ESV)

I don't know about you, but when I wait, I don't feel renewed. My strength actually dissipates. However, Isaiah reminds us that waiting for the Lord situates us to receive something we can't give ourselves. Jesus tells his disciples the same thing in the book of Acts:

> Do not leave Jerusalem, but wait for the gift
> my Father promised, which you have heard me
> speak about. For John baptized with water, but
> in a few days you will be baptized with the Holy
> Spirit. (1:4–5)

DAY
3

What does all this mean? Simply that what God does in you as you wait is just as important as—sometimes *more* important than—what you're waiting for.

We're *all* waiting for something in our lives, and it's common for us to live impulsively and reactively to make it appear. In this season, what would happen if you waited on God, even when it's uncomfortable? If you sat in his presence, your heart open to his will, ready to receive grace and strength?

When it feels as though he's abandoned you, may the peace of God sustain you in the waiting. I pray that even as you look ahead, longing for what's to come, you're able to rest in the goodness of God, knowing he's right beside you.

REFLECT

PREPARE: Spend two minutes in silence and stillness before God.

PRAYER FOR PRESENCE: Lord Jesus, in this moment of prayer, free me from the distractions of the day so that I may be deeply present to you and myself for the sake of the world around me.

DAY
3

——— SCRIPTURE | PSALM 39:4–7 ———

GUIDE: Waiting is an art that our impatient age has forgotten. It wants to break open the ripe fruit when it has hardly finished planting the shoot. But all too often the greedy eyes are only deceived; the fruit that seemed so precious is still green on the inside, and disrespectful hands ungratefully toss aside what has so disappointed them.[2]

—DIETRICH BONHOEFFER

QUESTION: During this season, in what ways is anxiety causing you to react instead of patiently waiting on the Lord? Spend a few minutes reflecting, praying, or writing what you sense God is speaking to your heart. If it's helpful, write out a simple prayer expressing your trust in his character, timing, and plans.

CLOSING PRAYER: Our Father in heaven, hallowed be your name, your kingdom come, your will be done, on earth as it is in heaven. Give us today our daily bread. And forgive us our debts, as we also have forgiven our debtors. And lead us not into temptation, but deliver us from the evil one.[3]

DAY
3

DAY 4

WAIT TRAINING

remember my first trip to Disney World. I was thirty-four years old. My wife and four-year-old daughter were with me. We had a wonderful time. We were able to secure Fast-Passes, which significantly lowered wait times for the rides. We had a great view of the fireworks. I wished upon a star. Just magical.

And then something happened.

We jumped onto a tram to take us back to the parking lot, and after a few minutes of easy travel, the vehicle stopped. Ten minutes later, an employee announced that it had broken down and we'd have to get off. And let me tell you, the most magical place on earth quickly became the most maddening place on earth.

People were angry. Some started booing as though we were at a ball game. The anger was palpable. It became apparent that the vast majority of people on that tram—myself included—had very little training in waiting.

It's remarkable how waiting reveals what's inside us. It unmasks our anger, anxieties, and frustrations unlike anything else. But what if there were a way to "wait train"? I think there is such a way. No gym membership is required. A few psalms will do.

WAITING WITH EXPECTATION

In Psalm 5:3, David says,

> In the morning, LORD, you hear my voice;
>> in the morning I lay my requests before you
>> and wait expectantly.

To wait expectantly is a great act of faith. It's a conviction that God is always at work (see John 5:17). If he never slumbers or sleeps, he is active in our lives and circumstances right now. In moments of waiting, God invites us to lay our requests before him. That simple act keeps us connected to him in challenging seasons.

WAITING WITH EMOTIONAL HONESTY

Another wait-training scripture is Psalm 40:1:

> I waited patiently for the LORD;
>   he turned to me and heard my cry.

To grow in our ability to wait on God requires us to be honest with him. In this psalm, David celebrates the good news that the Lord heard his cry. But before we can get to that point of celebration, we are called to name our desolation. One of the surprising sources of spiritual strength is found in our ability to be honest about our weaknesses. That is why the apostle Paul tells us,

> He said to me, "My grace is sufficient for you,
> for my power is made perfect in weakness."
> Therefore I will boast all the more gladly about
> my weaknesses, so that Christ's power may rest
> on me. That is why, for Christ's sake, I delight in
> weaknesses, in insults, in hardships, in persecu-
> tions, in difficulties. For when I am weak, then
> I am strong. (2 Corinthians 12:9–10)

To grow in wait training requires emotional honesty from us.

WAITING WITH ONE ANOTHER

One of the greatest sources of strength, especially in times of waiting, is a community of friends who wait with us. Waiting need not be an individual responsibility but rather a community burden. In fact, we can't understand the story of redemption in the Bible without seeing how waiting has always been a communal act.

The people of God wait *together*. When the Holy Spirit comes in the book of Acts, the community of Jesus followers are waiting *together*. The Psalms of Ascent (Psalms 120–134) are songs of the community trekking to Jerusalem. While it's easy to read them from an individual perspective, they were written with a waiting community in mind.

Advent is a time to increase our wait training. Yes, we look back at the earth-shattering moment when Jesus entered human history. Let's not forget that we need one another on the journey as we wait for Jesus to make all things new.

DAY
4

REFLECT

PREPARE: Spend two minutes in silence and stillness before God.

PRAYER FOR PRESENCE: Lord Jesus, in this moment, I believe you want to speak to me in a

deep and personal way. May I be attentive to your loving and merciful voice.

————— SCRIPTURE | ROMANS 5:1–5 —————

GUIDE: To follow God obediently requires believing that what is in store for all of us is bigger and better than our illusions of control and power—as individuals or as individual nations. Advent waiting is the time of relinquishing our desire to have outcomes our way and on our schedule.[1]

—JAMES A. KOWALSKI

QUESTION: How can you invite others into your waiting, and, conversely, how can you come alongside those seeking to be patient in their own waiting? Spend a few minutes reflecting, praying, or writing what you sense God is speaking to your heart.

CLOSING PRAYER: May the Lord bless us and keep us and cause his face to shine upon us from this day forth and forevermore. Amen.

WAITING FOR THE CHILD

n recent years, millions of people have become enamored with a child. The child came on the scene unexpectedly. Many were swept up by the impact the child made in such a short time. Just a few months after the child was revealed, countless people would have a replica of the child in their homes.

The child I'm referring to is Baby Yoda.

In the Star Wars hit show *The Mandalorian,* the Child (as Yoda is called) is special. Though small and unassuming, he wields mysterious powers. As a result, some seek to kill him. Others try to use him for their benefit. No matter where he goes, he astounds people and somehow becomes the center of attention.

If I hadn't mentioned Baby Yoda, you might have thought I was talking about baby Jesus, because the story is very similar.

The infant Jesus had power as the Son of God.

The infant Jesus was threatened to be killed.

The infant Jesus was the center of attention.

This Jesus was prophesied about many centuries before. The great prophet Isaiah foresaw a day when a child would come who would make all things new. Advent is the annual reminder that the hope we are all waiting for is not found in a strong economy, political leader, global power, or new accomplishment; it's found in the child, who was God.

Isaiah wrote,

> To us a child is born,
>> to us a son is given,
>> and the government will be on his shoulders.
> And he will be called
>> Wonderful Counselor, Mighty God,
>> Everlasting Father, Prince of Peace.
> Of the greatness of his government and peace
>> there will be no end.
>> (Isaiah 9:6–7)

DAY
5

As Isaiah looked ahead, he realized Jesus would not be an ordinary baby. Advent reminds us that this extraordinary child has come and that while we await his return, we can find comfort in five aspects of his power.

First, Jesus carries the government on his shoulders. All nations, thrones, and kingdoms are at his command. If there was ever a time when we needed this good news, it is now.

The political reality of our day has caused division, anger, and mistrust. We are told to believe that the government and the political world will be healed when our candidate gets elected or when our preferred political party has control. Isaiah reminds us that the only one who can bear the weight of the world on his shoulders is Jesus.

- *He* will be the one to bring justice and fairness.

- *He* will be the one to heal our divisions.

- *He* will be the one to make all things new.

DAY
5

Second, Jesus has wisdom for counseling us wonderfully. Isaiah reminds us that the Messiah is a wonderful counselor. God's counsel comes in many forms. I believe in counselors, therapists, social workers, and pastors. We need them all. In fact, a significant part of my spiritual-formation journey has included seasons of therapy. I've needed space to process when I've been stuck in my marriage and when high seasons of pastoral anxiety have come my way. This counsel often comes through others, but there is also a kind of counsel that only God can give us. The invitation of Advent is to open ourselves up to God's wisdom in Jesus Christ.

Third, Jesus has strength for upholding us. Though born as a small baby, he is almighty God. This is the mystery—the paradox—of Christianity: God humbled himself and housed

33

his infinite glory in the tiny frame of a child. As he grew, that power grew and made itself more visible:

- His might made sickness and disease flee.

- His might caused storms and winds to cease.

- His might put an end to death.

This same child, the Son of God, has the might to uphold *your* life.

Fourth, the Christ child has the tenderness and faithfulness of a father who never abandons his children. We often live as if God is angry at us or waiting for us to mess up. Jesus shows us what the Father is like: one who unconditionally cares for his children, even when they fumble and fail. He's the father who runs to greet prodigals on the long road home. Who wraps his arms around them and throws a party. Under his protection and care, we are safe.

Finally, Jesus calms the chaos of our lives. I don't know about you, but I desperately need peace. Maybe you need the assurance of hope that Jesus will make everything new. You're overwhelmed by the news, by the division, by the hostility. You need a revelation from God that Jesus is ultimately in control.

So if you feel uncertain about the future, look to the one who holds governments on his shoulders. If you need wisdom, sit with your wonderful counselor. If you feel weak, be upheld by almighty God. If you feel lost or ashamed, run to your compassionate Father. If your soul is churning with anxiety or hurt, seek refuge in the Prince of Peace.

Only in this child, the Son of God, can the deepest longings of your heart be met. This Advent season, go to Jesus.

REFLECT

PREPARE: Spend two minutes in silence and stillness before God.

PRAYER FOR PRESENCE: Lord Jesus, in this moment of prayer, free me from the distractions of the day so that I may be deeply present to you and myself for the sake of the world around me.

DAY
5

——— SCRIPTURE | 1 PETER 1:3–7 ———

GUIDE: Into this world, this demented inn, in which there is absolutely no room for Him at all, Christ has come uninvited. But because He cannot be at home in it, because He is out of place in it, and yet He must be in it, His place is with those others for whom there is no room. His place is with those who do not belong, who are rejected by power because they are regarded as weak, those who are discredited, who are denied the status of persons, tortured, exterminated. With those for whom there is no room, Christ is present in this world.[1]

—THOMAS MERTON

QUESTION: Which aspect of Jesus's power stands out to you? (1) The government resting on his shoulders, (2) Wonderful Counselor, (3) Mighty God, (4) Everlasting Father, (5) Prince of Peace. Spend a few minutes reflecting, praying, or writing what you sense God is speaking to your heart.

CLOSING PRAYER: Our Father in heaven, hallowed be your name, your kingdom come, your will be done, on earth as it is in heaven. Give us today our daily bread. And forgive us our debts, as we also have forgiven our debtors. And lead us not into temptation, but deliver us from the evil one.

DAY
5

THE FOOLISHNESS
OF WAITING

Have you ever delayed making a decision that seemed obvious but you ended up benefiting from waiting a little longer? When my wife, Rosie, and I were looking for a home to buy, we visited twenty open-house events. It was a very stressful season in our lives. One home in particular looked promising, but something about it just didn't sit right with us. After all the time and energy we'd spent searching, we decided to pass on it. It felt like foolishness to do so, but we waited a few more weeks. In the process, we discovered a house that would be exactly what we needed. Waiting on God can feel like foolishness, yet this "foolishness" can be a sign of great faith. And not just faith; it's an expression of God's way of life.

The Bible has much to say about fools. Most of the time, it's in a negative context, like in Proverbs, where the "fool" is someone who rejects wisdom, ignores God's guidance, and is on the path toward destruction.

But foolishness isn't *always* negative. In 1 Corinthians 3:18, Paul calls followers of Jesus to become "fools" in the eyes of the world—meaning that when we embrace God's wisdom, it's a counterintuitive approach that leads to life that confounds conventional wisdom. That is where *waiting* comes in. In an age of instant gratification, to suspend our in-the-moment desires can feel foolish.

In fact, the entire Bible is written in the context of a people who are waiting. When God promises Abraham a son, the man has to wait twenty-five years to see it fulfilled. The Israelites suffered as slaves in Egypt, waiting for more than four hundred years for deliverance. After establishing a great kingdom, only to be carried off into exile, they again waited for God to step in on their behalf. In the Gospels, God's people waited once more—this time for a messiah who could free them from foreign oppression. They longed for God to set things right.

DAY
6

In Luke 2, the infant Jesus was brought to the temple to be circumcised, which was part of Jewish religion and culture. Mary and Joseph went down to the temple to have a baby-dedication service and presented their firstborn to the Lord. When they arrived at the temple, they encountered a man named Simeon, who was waiting for them.

If you could summarize Simeon's life in a word, it would be *waiting*. Simeon was a righteous and devout man. God had promised him he would not die until he had seen the

Christ. Some traditions say he was more than one hundred years old, and while the Bible doesn't specify his age, it's clear that he'd been waiting a long time for the coming Messiah. Right when Mary and Joseph appeared in the temple court, Simeon knew who they were and that the baby they held was the Messiah. Taking Jesus into his arms, Simeon prayed,

> Sovereign Lord, as you have promised,
>> you may now dismiss your servant in peace.
> For my eyes have seen your salvation,
>> which you have prepared in the sight of all
>>> nations:
> a light for revelation to the Gentiles,
>> and the glory of your people Israel.
>>> (verses 29–32)

DAY
6

It was the moment of his life, yet for countless years, Simeon probably felt as though his waiting was in vain. Interestingly, his name means "God has heard." Can you imagine the anger and resentment he might have carried? Clinging to God's promise, but feeling like he's distant and deaf? What happens when your name means one thing but your life tells a different story?

As decades passed, I'm sure Simeon felt foolish. However, even in the man's discomfort, God slowly expanded his capacity to wait. Though Simeon's increasing longing felt bitter, it made the delivered promise that much sweeter. I love that although he had been waiting for years, Simeon was sensitive to God's leading. In verse 27, it says, "Moved by the Spirit, he went into the temple courts." How easy it would have been to assume that day was just like the rest: fruitless, aimless, mundane. Instead, he was expectant and obedient.

So, what does it mean to wait for God? Simeon shows us. Here are four observations.

1. ALTHOUGH SIMEON WAITED A LONG TIME, HE DIDN'T LEAVE

He was rooted, his eyes fixed on God. When we wait for the Lord, it reminds us we are not the center of the universe. It's humbling to stay put when easier options are available. Those who wait on God give up their right to take charge and call the shots. A great question to ask during Advent is, Are you willing to stay planted, even when it's difficult, in order to wait on God's timing?

2. SIMEON REFUSED TO FOLLOW FALSE MESSIAHS

During his more than one hundred years of life, how easy it would have been to settle for another leader or figure, especially when God's promised Messiah hadn't arrived. How effortless to chase after another person he could see, hear, and touch. After all, the first century was filled with so-called

DAY
6

messiahs offering to rescue Israel. But Simeon kept his eyes on the promise. And he waited.

How often do we hastily set our hearts on someone or something, thinking it will save us? Whether with romantic relationships or political leaders, we look to others with messianic expectation. Panic leads to impulsive decisions, but if, like Simeon, we wait for the Lord, we'll discover the goodness of his plan.

3. SIMEON WAITED WITH A DISCERNING HEART

If we're not careful, long periods of waiting lead to spiritual sleepiness. It's easy to check out. To slip into autopilot. Henri Nouwen noted, "Waiting patiently is not like waiting for the bus to come, the rain to stop, or the sun to rise. It is an active waiting in which we live the present moment to the full in order to find there the signs of the One we are waiting for."[1] Waiting patiently means paying attention to what is happening right before our eyes, being eager to discover how God is working.

DAY
6

4. SIMEON WAITED IN COMMUNITY

Again, waiting is easier when we have someone to do it with. In this passage, we discover Simeon wasn't alone:

> There was also a prophet, Anna, the daughter of
> Penuel, of the tribe of Asher. She was very old;
> she had lived with her husband seven years after
> her marriage, and then was a widow until she
> was eighty-four. She never left the temple but
> worshiped night and day, fasting and praying.
> (verses 36–37)

We don't know the extent of Simeon and Anna's interactions, but they waited together. We all need a community to belong to that shares our hope for the future and helps us stay faithful in the present.

As Simeon waited, God worked in him. I love how Eugene Peterson paraphrased Romans 8 in *The Message*:

> Waiting does not diminish us, any more than
> waiting diminishes a pregnant mother. We are
> enlarged in the waiting. We, of course, don't see
> what is enlarging us. But the longer we wait, the
> larger we become, and the more joyful our ex-
> pectancy. (verses 24–25)

In our waiting, typically we ask, "God, why is this taking so long?" There's a biblical precedent for crying out, "How long, Lord?" But there are also times when a better question is "God, what are you trying to form in me?" Perhaps he cares about who you're becoming *in the process* more than he does about rushing you to your destination. Sometimes his message to us is "Don't waste your wait."

REFLECT

PREPARE: Spend two minutes in silence and stillness before God.

PRAYER FOR PRESENCE: Lord Jesus, in this moment of prayer, free me from the distractions of the day so that I may be deeply present to you and myself for the sake of the world around me.

——— SCRIPTURE | PSALM 31:21–24 ———

DAY
6

GUIDE: Advent is about learning to wait. It is about not having to know exactly what is coming tomorrow, only that whatever it is, it is of the essence of sanctification for us. Every piece of it, some hard, some uplifting, is a sign of the work of God alive in us. We are becoming as we go. We learn in Advent to stay in the present, knowing that only the present well lived can possibly lead us to the fullness of life. . . .

Advent relieves us of our commitment to the frenetic in a fast-paced world. It slows us down. It makes us think. It makes us look beyond today to the "great tomorrow" of life. Without Advent, moved only by the race to nowhere that exhausts the world around us, we could be so frantic with trying to consume and control this life that we fail to develop within ourselves a taste for the spirit that does not die and will not slip through our fingers like melted snow.[2]

—JOAN CHITTISTER

QUESTION: How can you lean more into community in this season to help you patiently wait on God? Spend a few minutes reflecting, praying, or writing what you sense God is speaking to your heart.

CLOSING PRAYER: Our Father in heaven, hallowed be your name, your kingdom come, your will be done, on earth as it is in heaven. Give us today our daily bread. And forgive us our debts, as we also have forgiven our debtors. And lead us not into temptation, but deliver us from the evil one.

PART TWO

PEACEMAKING

JESUS OR HEROD

Advent presents us with two ways of being in the world: like the unarmed infant Messiah, Jesus, or like the armed and fearful leader Herod. When Jesus was born, the gospel writers contrasted these two approaches to securing peace. The question for every one of us is this: Which way will we choose?

Lately, I've reflected on my tendency to be self-protective and fearful (aka, like Herod). My self-protectiveness gets expressed when congregants want to offer honest perspectives on what it's like to be part of our congregation. Or it gets triggered when Rosie offers feedback about the frenetic pace of life I can sometimes succumb to. When that happens, I emotionally shut down. I close myself off, afraid of having to come to terms with not having it all together. By the grace of God, I have once again come to realize that the impotent way of Herod does little to contribute to true shalom and human flourishing. One of the times this realization hits me afresh is when the season of Advent comes around. I'm confronted by the inner Herod that dwells within me.

This Advent season, I've been asking this question: *Is my default posture to those who threaten me one of animosity or one of kingdom love?*

When God entered the world in the person of Jesus, he came in the most surprising and subversive method possible. In coming as an infant, unarmed and vulnerable, he established the way of the kingdom from the onset. The kingdom is not characterized by fear, self-interest, or violence; it's defined by vulnerable trust and supernatural love.

DAY
7

This love isn't passive or weak. Rather, Jesus came to disarm Herod and the ways of his violent kingdom. Though love does not use force through violence, as it silently infiltrates the world, it is an unstoppable force. It transforms enemies.

On the contrary, Herod longed only to *defeat* his enemies. In his insecure and fearful way, he preemptively wiped out anyone who threatened his kingdom. Herod essentially said, "Let's rid ourselves of these imminent threats before we fall into their hands." The spirit of Herod permeates our country—even our Christian churches and institutions.

When will we see that the way of vulnerable love is the way of Jesus's kingdom?

When will we realize that to subdue Herod with Herodian tactics further perpetuates violence and works against the world we truly long for?

When will we embrace the supernatural truth that perfect love casts out fear? Until we do so, we are all little Herods protecting our present with no regard for our future.

Perhaps the most insidious consequence of the way of Herod is the crushing weight that marks and diminishes our souls.

Herod and his violent methods know nothing about the path to peace. The way of Jesus and his kingdom is better. This Advent season, will you courageously entrust your life to the one who offers true peace?

REFLECT

PREPARE: Spend two minutes in silence and stillness before God.

PRAYER FOR PRESENCE: Lord Jesus, in this moment of prayer, free me from the distractions of the day so that I may be deeply present to you and myself for the sake of the world around me.

——— SCRIPTURE | PSALM 46:1–10 ———

GUIDE: [Waiting] as a people of nonviolence in a world of war, you'll know [that] Advent is patience. It is how God has made us the people of promise in a world of impatience. And Christ has made that possible for us to live patiently in a world of impatience.[1]

—STANLEY HAUERWAS

QUESTION: In your life right now, what is an area in which you're embracing the way of Herod—perhaps in a relationship, mindset, or habit? How can you surrender this area into the powerful hands of Jesus, trusting him to protect you and provide for you?

CLOSING PRAYER: Our Father in heaven, hallowed be your name, your kingdom come, your will be done, on earth as it is in heaven. Give us today our daily bread. And forgive us our debts, as we also have forgiven our debtors. And lead us not into temptation, but deliver us from the evil one.

SHALOMING THE WORLD

A few years ago, I visited a friend in Fort Collins, Colorado. He took me to a place called Horsetooth Reservoir. It was one of the most sacred moments of my life.

The air was crisp, the sight was serene, and when I got to a certain spot near the water, it was as silent as any place I had ever been. For about two whole minutes, there was nothing but stillness.

That moment, in a word, could be described as *peace*.

We all want this. We all need this. But there's another image that I think captures what biblical peace really is.

When I was a teenager, my brother and I had a small basketball hoop that we attached to our bedroom door. We would play, and from time to time, our father would join us.

The hoop was usually in our bedroom, but when we needed more space (and when Mom wasn't home), we would bring it to the living room.

However, in the living room, my mother had all kinds of figurines. And one day as we were playing, the ball hit one of her favorite dog figurines, shattering it into pieces. The fear of the Lord came over us. In that instant, we realized that breaking the figurine was quickly going to lead to a greater, more personal brokenness if my mother found out.

So right then, we began to work for peace.

In the Bible, the word *shalom* is one of the more common (and powerful) words used for "peace." *Shalom* means "harmony, wholeness, inner stillness, being put back together." It's more than merely a description of how things are, or how they should be. *Shalom* is a verb. An action. A way of life.

In that moment of anxiety, my father, brother, and I began to work together like a group of surgeons performing emergency surgery. With glue in hand and a set of eyes looking out the window for Mom's arrival, we *shalomed* the little dog together.

More than an idyllic landscape does, this makeshift operation captures what peace is. It's more than the absence of conflict, adversity, and pain. As Advent reminds us, Jesus came *into* a broken world to make it whole. Peace is restoring wholeness to something that is broken.

And when I think about our world, there are a lot of

things that are shattered. Maybe we long for peace in our families but decades of dysfunction have drained our hope. The holidays can feel like a dagger plunged into old relational wounds, where instead of peace, we experience pain. Rather than putting things back together, we're reminded that everything has fallen apart.

Or maybe we're longing to see peace in the world. Whether it's the heartbreaking violence in the Middle East, gun violence in the United States, or the vitriol of political institutions, we long to see our world made whole.

How should we respond to a world so broken? How do we satisfy our longing for shalom?

This longing should lead us, in small and big ways, to turn *shalom* into a verb. We can all start the journey of shaloming the world. We can patiently take the fragments in our homes and neighborhoods and, in the name of Jesus, work toward healing and peace.

DAY
8

As long as we see peace as a state of being "out there," there will be no urgency to join God in healing the world. But we are invited to become people who "peace" the world together.

REFLECT

PREPARE: Spend two minutes in silence and stillness before God.

PRAYER FOR PRESENCE: Lord Jesus, in this moment, I believe you want to speak to me in a deep and personal way. May I be attentive to your loving and merciful voice.

SCRIPTURE | LUKE 2:8-14

GUIDE: First keep peace with yourself, then you will be able to bring peace to others. The peaceful do more good than the learned. While the passionate turn even good to evil and are quick to believe evil, the peaceful, being good themselves, turn all things to good.

The man who is at perfect ease is never suspicious, but the disturbed and discontented spirit is upset by many suspicions. He neither rests himself nor permits others to do so. He often says what ought not to be said and leaves undone what ought to be done. He is concerned with the duties of others but neglects his own. Now, all our peace in this life is found in humbly enduring suffering, rather than in being free from it. He who knows best how to suffer will enjoy the greater peace, because he is the conqueror of himself, the master of the world, a friend of Christ, and an heir of heaven.[1]

—THOMAS À KEMPIS

QUESTION: What is one small way you can "shalom" the world around you in your family, home, neighborhood, or workplace?

CLOSING PRAYER: May the Lord bless us and keep us and cause his face to shine upon us from this day forth and forevermore. Amen.

DAY
8

DISRUPTING FALSE PEACE

When I first became a Christian, my pastor said something you've probably heard: "In life, you are either in a storm, coming out of a storm, or going into a storm." He was spot-on. No matter how smart, wealthy, or powerful you are, you will experience storms in life.

And one of the most common types of storms you'll encounter is conflict with others. It's inevitable: You're either in a conflict, just emerging from a conflict, or about to head into a conflict. It might be with someone at church, your spouse, your significant other, your co-worker, or your child, but rest assured, relational turbulence is coming. I say this not to discourage you but to prepare you.

Truthfully, few of us have been equipped to work through conflict in a way that brings true peace. A cursory glance at the world reveals a similar reality: nations stockpiling weapons of mass destruction, gang violence, domestic abuse, sexual assault, racism-fueled violence, terrorism, and the list goes on.

Advent is a welcome reminder that in addition to bringing peace to our world, God also invites us to join him in that effort. According to Jesus, God's kingdom is made known when peacemakers are present. As followers of Jesus, we are invited to make the world more whole.

In my book *The Narrow Path,* I talk about how we mistake peace*keeping* (being nice and trying not to rock the boat) for what Jesus teaches: peace*making.* People keep the peace to avoid making others uncomfortable. This is appeasing others out of fear. Let me give you some examples:

DAY
9

- You're mad at your spouse, who comes home late from work day after day, but you say nothing. Why? Because you think you're being like Christ by absorbing your frustration. But as your anger builds, you're tempted to become passive-aggressive, give the silent treatment, or explode. That's false peace.

- Let's say you hear your co-workers tearing down your boss. You go along with it because you're afraid to speak up. You don't want to navigate an awkward moment. That's false peace.

- You go to dinner with a group of friends. Things are tight financially, so you order just an appetizer. Meanwhile, the other nine people order appetizers, steak, wine, and dessert. When the bill comes, someone says, "Let's divide up the bill equally. It will take forever to figure it out." Everyone agrees. You are dying on the inside but won't say anything. That's false peace.

- You think your boyfriend is irresponsible, but you feel bad for him: *He's already had so much pain in his life. I can't add to that.* So you avoid the truth about the negative ways his behavior affects you. Your relationship slowly withers. That's false peace.

As I continued to write in *The Narrow Path,*

Here's the thing with peace*keeping:* sooner or later, it brings chaos—not peace—into your life. Peace*making* is quite different. Peacemakers don't avoid conflict; in fact, sometimes peacemaking *creates* it. We see this with Jesus. As the epitome of love, he wasn't always nice—at least not in the way modern people visualize niceness.

On several occasions, he burst into the temple and flipped tables over because poor, vulnerable people were being taken advantage of (see Matthew 21:12). When he saw the Pharisees putting yokes of religious condemnation on people, he confronted the religious leaders with harsh words.

As Jesus's life reveals, peacemaking is often met with resistance. Paradoxically, to make peace means entering a war. The peace of God uproots the exploitative schemes of evil, and that evil won't back down without a fight.[1]

As Jesus's bold actions show us, we can't avoid, ignore, or deny our way into true peace. Jesus did not say, "Blessed are the peace wishers." Or the peace hopers or the peace dreamers or the peace lovers or the peace talkers.

No, "Blessed are the peace*makers,* for they will be called children of God" (Matthew 5:9). This Advent season, don't shy away from this high calling. Peacemaking is rarely convenient or comfortable, but as you seek to bring God's shalom into the world, his blessing will rest upon you.

REFLECT

PREPARE: Spend two minutes in silence and stillness before God.

PRAYER FOR PRESENCE: Lord Jesus, in this moment of prayer, free me from the distractions of the day so that I may be deeply present to you and myself for the sake of the world around me.

——— SCRIPTURE | MATTHEW 5:3–12 ———

GUIDE: *"Blessed are the peacemakers: for they shall be called the children of God."* The followers of Jesus have been called to peace. When he called them they found their peace, for he is their peace. But now they are told that they must not only *have* peace but *make* it. And to that end they renounce all violence and tumult. In the cause of Christ nothing is to be gained by such methods. His kingdom is one of peace, and the mutual greeting of his flock is a greeting of peace. His disciples keep the peace by choosing to endure suffering themselves rather than inflict it on others. They maintain fellowship where others would break it off. They renounce all self-assertion, and quietly suffer in the face of hatred and wrong. In so doing they overcome evil with good, and establish the peace of God in the midst of a world of war and hate. But nowhere will that peace be more manifest than where they meet the wicked in peace and are ready to suffer at their hands. The peacemakers will carry the cross with their Lord, for it was on the cross that peace was made. Now that they are partners in Christ's work of reconciliation, they are called the sons of God as he is the Son of God.[2]

—Dietrich Bonhoeffer

QUESTION: How is God inviting you to make peace in the world around you? What is one simple way you can say yes to his invitation today?

CLOSING PRAYER: Our Father in heaven, hallowed be your name, your kingdom come, your will be done, on earth as it is in heaven. Give us today our daily bread. And forgive us our debts, as we also have forgiven our debtors. And lead us not into temptation, but deliver us from the evil one.

DAY

9

PEACE BEYOND UNDERSTANDING

The "Miracle on the Hudson" is a wonderful New York story. In January 2009, a US Airways plane took off from LaGuardia Airport. Two minutes after takeoff, a flock of Canada geese slammed into the engines. One pilot in my church said that if one goose hit an engine, that would be very serious. In this case, it was a flock.

This called for an emergency landing. Enter Captain Chesley "Sully" Sullenberger.

Sullenberger realized that he needed to land the plane immediately, but he could not make it back to the airport. In a conversation with air traffic control, they discussed landing on one of the highways, but that would be too dangerous and there wasn't enough time.

The only viable option—and the only place in New York

City long, wide, and smooth enough to attempt a landing of a large modern jet airliner—was the Hudson River.

Thankfully, Captain Sullenberger was trained for that specific kind of crisis. He needed to act fast. What's staggering about the entire event is that there were only 208 seconds between the plane hitting the geese and the landing on the water. Less than four minutes. And in that time frame, Sully landed it safely.[1]

Of all the great things about this story, what stands out to me is the calm that Sully had. The last words he spoke to air traffic control were calm (urgent, yes, but still calm). What he said was, "We're gonna be in the Hudson."[2] In a time of crisis, he was not paralyzed by anxiety. Remarkably, everyone on board was safely rescued.

If I were Captain Sullenberger's copilot, my last words would not be so calm. I imagine they would be something like, "We just hit a flock of birds. Both engines are gone. We're going down! Do you hear me, tower? We're going down! We're headed for the Hudson River! We're all gonna die! Say your prayers. Tell my wife I love her, 'cause we're all gonna die. Aaahhhhhhhh!!!" (Come on, you would say pretty much the same thing.)

This story resonates with us because it has a happy ending. But it also resonates with us (especially as we talk about Christian spirituality) because it's an illustration about responding to crisis and difficulty. One way to measure the nature of our faith is to observe our responses to crisis. Difficulty reveals what's going on inside us.

And if we look inside our hearts, what many of us find is anxiety. In my early twenties, I experienced a series of anxiety attacks with causes that ranged from relationship stress to uncertainty about my future. Even if you've never had an anxiety attack, we all know what it's like to carry excessive worry and stress.

The story of Advent is about a God who is *with* us in our times of adversity. His presence brings peace. Many people need this peace today but aren't sure where to find it, and it feels as though fear is winning. What if I told you that like Captain Sullenberger trained for *his* moment of difficulty, you can train for yours?

In Philippians 4:6–7, Paul says,

> Do not be anxious about anything, but in every situation, by prayer and petition, with thanksgiving, present your requests to God. And the peace of God, which transcends all understanding, will guard your hearts and your minds in Christ Jesus.

When Paul wrote that, he wasn't trying to land a plane; he was lying in prison. He knew about stress and anxiety. Here are three channels he gives for receiving the peace of Christ:

1. Prayer
2. Petition
3. Thanksgiving

This isn't a recipe, as if an ounce of prayer, a pinch of petition, and a spoonful of thanksgiving will magically transform our lives. However, Paul named a few practices that, over time, help us live from a different center. Think of Advent as a season of training:

First, commit to prayer this Advent. When you bring your full self to God, paying attention to his presence, you position yourself to receive peace.

Second, commit to pouring out requests to God. Lift your longings, desires, fears, and requests to him. Like a good father, he delights in hearing your requests and meeting your needs. Resist the impulse to be independent; you were made to lean wholeheartedly on the Creator. To raise your burdens to God is to open yourself to his power.

Third, Advent is a time for thanksgiving. As you name the gifts you've received, even in difficult situations, you anchor your heart, mind, and soul in God's goodness. You remind yourself that he is faithful. You rest in his promises.

Don't wait until your darkest moment to prepare your heart. Start now, even in little ways. Pray, enjoying the presence of God. Petition, seeking the help of God. And give thanks, declaring the goodness of God. As you do, you will discover a peace that transcends any circumstance.

REFLECT

PREPARE: Spend two minutes in silence and stillness before God.

PRAYER FOR PRESENCE: Lord Jesus, in this moment, I believe you want to speak to me in a deep and personal way. May I be attentive to your loving and merciful voice.

———SCRIPTURE | MATTHEW 25:31–45———

GUIDE: The longer we meditate, the more we become aware that the source of our new-found calm in our daily lives is precisely the life of God within us. The degree of peace we possess is directly proportional to our awareness of this fact of life, a fact of human consciousness, common to every man and every woman in the world. But to realize this fact as a present reality in our lives, we have to decide that we want to be at peace. This is the reason for the psalmist's saying: "Be still and know that I am God" (Ps. 46.10).

This deep inner peacefulness is in a sense more freely available for us today than it was for the Hebrew poet who wrote that psalm, even if our problems are greater and our pace of life faster than his were; and this is because of the great fact of Jesus.[3]

—JOHN MAIN

QUESTION: Spend a few minutes practicing the three training methods: prayer, petition, and

DAY

10

66

thanksgiving. In a journal or out loud, bring your full self to God.

CLOSING PRAYER: May the Lord bless us and keep us and cause his face to shine upon us from this day forth and forevermore. Amen.

DAY
10

GLORY TO GOD, PEACE TO US

very year, our church staff has an annual Christmas party. It's always a good time. We have competitions, food, and, of course, karaoke. It's one of the highlights of the season for me. You see, I love singing. And even though I can't sing *well,* I love doing it anyway.

I've done songs by Aerosmith, Lionel Richie, Bon Jovi, and Ricky Martin. (If you're interested, yes, I do birthday parties, bar mitzvahs, weddings, you name it.) One of the funny things about karaoke is that even though the words are in front of you, it's easy to mess up the lyrics. To mess up the flow. To make up stuff that's not even part of the song. I have a tendency to do this, which drives Rosie crazy.

But there's another problem we have when it comes to songs about God and the spiritual life: Even though we sing the right words, we don't always *live* those words out.

In the gospel of Luke, we learn a simple song that's easy to remember yet difficult to apply:

> Suddenly a great company of the heavenly host appeared with the angel, praising God and saying,
>
> "Glory to God in the highest heaven,
>   and on earth peace to those on whom
>   his favor rests."
>
> (2:13–14)

Pay close attention to the lyrics. The song is about two things:

1. Glory to God.
2. Peace to us.

DAY
11

If you're like me, it's so easy to sing the words "glory to God" while living for my own glory. In Scripture, *glory* refers to something heavy, or weighty—not in terms of pounds, but in terms of splendor. Grandness. Greatness. Significance. That's glory. When we hear someone play an instrument or sing a song and their very presence fills the space, we say, "That was glorious." It is a natural response to seeing something magnificent.

The Westminster Catechism offers this famous question and answer:

> Q: What is the chief end of man?
> A: Man's chief end is to glorify God, and to enjoy him forever.[1]

But often that is not how we live. The problem is, when we attempt to *gain* glory instead of *give* glory, we are crushed under its weight. Only God is powerful and worthy enough to sustain worship, and we experience the deepest joy when we marvel at him. We were made for this. It's easy to live our lives striving for success and significance, but in so doing, we find ourselves exhausted, chasing something that is unattainable.

In the social media world we live in, we are trained to make much of ourselves, but that warps our souls and depletes our joy. According to a 2016 study published in *Psychological Science,* scientists at the University of California, Los Angeles, found that when teenagers see large numbers of "likes" on their own photos or the photos of their peers, their brains react in the same way they would when eating chocolate or winning money.[2] However, when they don't accrue likes, the opposite effect takes place.

We are hungry for glory, and the only one who can satisfy that hunger is God himself. The angels in Luke's gospel understood this. They knew that once we get the glory part right, peace is sure to follow.

God's peace is for those who let go of personal glory. This Advent, what would it look like to focus less on yourself and more on Jesus? Don't fall into the trap of self-obsession, for in the end, acclaim and status are fickle and fading. Instead, fix your attention and affection on the one the angels have been singing about since before the world began. When you join in *that* song, your heart will be flooded with inexplicable peace as your eyes feast on a glory so weighty that you can (and will) spend eternity gazing upon it with wonder.

REFLECT

PREPARE: Spend two minutes in silence and stillness before God.

PRAYER FOR PRESENCE: Lord Jesus, in this moment, I believe you want to speak to me in a deep and personal way. May I be attentive to your loving and merciful voice.

———— SCRIPTURE | ISAIAH 9:2–7 ————

DAY
11

GUIDE: Keep your eyes on the Prince of Peace, the one who doesn't cling to his divine power; the one who refuses to turn stones into bread, jump from great heights, and rule with great power; the one who says, "Blessed are the poor, the gentle, those who mourn, and those who hunger and thirst for righteousness; blessed are the merciful, the pure in heart, the peacemakers and those who are persecuted in the cause of uprightness" (see Matt. 5:3–11); the one who touches the lame, the crippled, and the blind; the one who speaks words of forgiveness and encouragement; the one who dies alone, rejected and despised. Keep your eyes on him who becomes poor with the poor, weak with the weak, and who is rejected with the rejected. He is the source of all peace.[3]

—Henri Nouwen

QUESTION: Reflect on a time when you experienced God's glory in an especially powerful way. Where were you, and what happened? Thank God for that experience and invite him to show you more of himself today.

CLOSING PRAYER: May the Lord bless us and keep us and cause his face to shine upon us from this day forth and forevermore. Amen.

RECEIVING PEACE

Advent is an ideal time to clarify our vision about what God is like. The way we think about him will lead us to either peace or instability. Advent boldly declares that God arrives in the form of a human infant and, through his presence, ushers in a kind of peace that heals the world.

Yet this is not how most people think about God. I came across a survey done some years ago by Baylor University. The survey was about America's ideas of God. Although 95 percent of Americans say they believe in God, the researchers concluded that Americans have four very different conceptions of who he is:

1. the authoritative God, who both judges and is closely engaged in the world

2. the benevolent God, who is engaged but non-judgmental
3. the critical God, who happens to be judgmental but disengaged
4. the distant God, who is neither engaged nor judgmental and could care less about what humans worry about[1]

When *you* think about God, do you see him as distant or involved? Critical or benevolent? Authoritative or laid-back? In your view, does he want a piece of you, or does he want to give you peace?

The degree to which peace is part of your view of God is the degree to which you will experience the abundant life Jesus offers you. Christianity reveals a God of grace and peace, yet we have a hard time accepting this because we carry deep shame about things we've said and done. It's one thing to agree cognitively that God brings peace; it's another thing entirely to receive it. To live from a secure place. To trust in the character and heart of God. To believe he is for us.

We believe that our sin is too deep for God to forgive. In an attempt to atone for our own shortcomings, we disqualify ourselves from grace and peace. We live according to the script of legalism, which seeks to earn God's favor. But as Tim Keller reminds us, "Religion operates on the principle 'I obey—therefore I am accepted by God.' But the operating principle of the gospel is 'I am accepted by God through what Christ has done—therefore I obey.'"[2] We can never

74

make things right in our own strength. Grace is a gift, not something to earn.

Some of us might carry pride because of accomplishments or perceived righteousness. Chances are, if we're out of touch with our need for grace, we're probably out of touch with the depth of our brokenness. The people in Scripture who forfeited God's grace and peace the most were the religious leaders. Jesus explained to them, "I didn't come for those that are well, but for the sick" (see Mark 2:17). What he meant was that only those who recognize their need for God will find him.

So, how do we live our lives from a place of grace and peace? How do we enjoy doing that? How do we display it?

The answer is simple but challenging: We position ourselves to receive it. One of the things I loved doing while growing up was going to baseball games with my dad. Every time we went to the stadium, he would tell me to bring my glove. Whether we were sitting high up in the stands or right by the field, he'd say, "Always have your glove ready. You never know when it's going to come your way."

DAY
12

You can't force the ball to come to you, but you can place yourself before it to receive it. The same is true with peace. You can't manufacture it. Or buy it. Or force it. All you can do is ready yourself to catch it.

How do you catch it? By recognizing that peace is not just an emotional state of being; it's a Person. Advent announces the arrival of Peace. The arrival of the Messiah. The arrival of God.

This Advent, make room for Jesus. Prepare your heart to receive him. Come back to the Cross and Resurrection, where you're reminded that God offered himself for you. He's done everything he can to give you grace and peace.

REFLECT

PREPARE: Spend two minutes in silence and stillness before God.

PRAYER FOR PRESENCE: Lord Jesus, in this moment, I believe you want to speak to me in a deep and personal way. May I be attentive to your loving and merciful voice.

——— SCRIPTURE | MATTHEW 6:25-32 ———

GUIDE: Soberly, when our trust is in things that are absolutely beyond any risk or threat, and we have learned from good sources, including our own experience, that those things are *there,* anxiety is just groundless and pointless. It occurs only as a hangover of bad habits established when we were trusting things—like human approval and wealth—that were certain to let us down. Now our strategy should be one of resolute rejection of worry, while we concentrate on the future in hope and with prayer and on the past with thanks-giving.[3]

—DALLAS WILLARD

QUESTION: What hinders you from receiving God's grace and peace? Is it legalism (trying to earn his love), pride (feeling little need for his love), guilt (feeling unworthy of his love), or something else?

CLOSING PRAYER: May the Lord bless us and keep us and cause his face to shine upon us from this day forth and forevermore. Amen.

DAY

12

PART THREE

REJOICING

INCREASING YOUR JOY

n a popular show called *Sparking Joy with Marie Kondo,* the host—a Japanese organizing consultant and author—helps people declutter their lives and homes. In every episode, she asks a simple question to help people decide whether to keep something or not: Does it spark joy? She'll have someone pile all their clothes in one room, then pick up one item at a time, deciding if it brings joy to their life or not.

Now, let me say that I need to do this exercise. I have a lot of stuff to get rid of. Marie's question about an item's ability to produce joy is valid; however, it's not a good philosophy for *all* of life. Evaluating everything in your life based on its joy yield can lead to some bad decisions. You might look at your dog, your husband, your kids, your job, your whatever, and start getting rid of stuff if it doesn't always produce good feelings.

We need a better understanding of joy. A biblical perspective. The joy of our world is based on circumstances and preferences. We think, *if* this happens, *then* I'll be joyful. But the if-then principle rarely works over the long haul. Many of our hopes, which we imagine will grant happiness if we attain them, never happen. If our dreams don't pan out as planned, is joy then impossible?

What we need is something deeper. Something more consistent. Something long-lasting. The joy found in the story of the Bible is more than a happy feeling. It includes feelings, of course, but it is not dependent on them.

In Scripture, true joy flows from the life of God, yet this can feel elusive. Of all the Advent themes, living joyfully seems most challenging. It can be hard to have joy when there's sorrow around us and we see the pain of others. We can't just whip up joy at a moment's notice or force our emotions into action. In the Bible, joy is not something we create so much as it is something we receive. Joy is not a switch we can turn on but rather a state of being we can cultivate as we spend time with God.

Being in his presence is the place to start. As you allow his light to break into your life, darkness dissipates. That is what Isaiah is getting at in this passage:

> The people walking in darkness
>   have seen a great light;
> on those living in the land of deep darkness
>   a light has dawned.

You have enlarged the nation
and increased their joy;
they rejoice before you
as people rejoice at the harvest.
(Isaiah 9:2–3)

That is the core message of Advent. The joy we want will never come from our ability to work it up; it comes from God's willingness to work it in. In this season, you are invited to experience joy in his presence. Release yourself from the pressure to produce your own happiness. Your joy comes from *his* faithfulness, seen in the face of Jesus, whose birth angels announced as good news that brings exceeding joy.

DAY
13

Wherever you are or whatever you're experiencing right now, my prayer is that God's joy would increase in your life as you rest in his presence.

REFLECT

PREPARE: Spend two minutes in silence and stillness before God.

PRAYER FOR PRESENCE: Lord Jesus, in this moment of prayer, free me from the distractions of the day so that I may be deeply present to you and myself for the sake of the world around me.

GUIDE: Joy is not a requirement of Christian discipleship; it is a consequence. It is not what we have to acquire in order to experience life in Christ; it is what comes to us when we are walking in the way of faith and obedience. . . .

We try to get [joy] through entertainment. We pay someone to make jokes, tell stories, perform dramatic actions, sing songs. We buy the vitality of another's imagination to divert and enliven our own poor lives. The enormous entertainment industry in America is a sign of the depletion of joy in our culture. Society is a bored, gluttonous king employing a court jester to divert it after an overindulgent meal. But that kind of joy never penetrates our lives, never changes our basic constitution. The effects are extremely temporary; a few quiet minutes, a few hours, a few days at most. When we run out of money, the joy trickles away. We cannot make ourselves joyful. Joy cannot be commanded, purchased or arranged.

But there is something we can do. We can decide to live in response to the abundance of God and not under the dictatorship of our own poor needs. We can decide to live in the environment of a living God and not our own dying selves. We can decide to center ourselves in the God who generously gives and not in our own egos which greedily grab. One of the certain consequences of such a life is joy, the kind expressed in Psalm 126.[1]

—EUGENE PETERSON

QUESTION: In what ways are you seeking joy in temporary things? How might you position yourself to receive the joy of the Lord during this Advent season?

CLOSING PRAYER: Our Father in heaven, hallowed be your name, your kingdom come, your will be done, on earth as it is in heaven. Give us today our daily bread. And forgive us our debts, as we also have forgiven our debtors. And lead us not into temptation, but deliver us from the evil one.

DAY
13

COMPLETE JOY

When you picture Jesus, what expression is on his face? Perhaps, like many people, you see him as melancholy, severe, or scowling. Just think about how he is portrayed in art. Usually he is very serious. Stoic. Intense. Sadly, we rarely associate Jesus with joy. We can't afford to overlook the joyful nature he possesses, because—like all his traits—it's a key part of him.

When Jesus described the kingdom in Matthew 22:1–14, he called it a banquet and a wedding: two environments of great joy. He was certainly acquainted with pain, but he lived with profound joy, saying to his followers, "I have told you this so that my joy may be in you and that your joy may be complete" (John 15:11). Jesus was filled with joy, and he wants *our* lives to be marked with it.

Over the past week, I asked people on Facebook and

around church about their joy levels. I want to ask you as well: When you consider your life today, are you filled with joy? Or does it feel elusive?

The responses have been fascinating. Many people have said, "I'd be more joyful if [insert life goal or dream] happened." Or "I'd be joyful if I met someone." Or "I'd be joyful if I got a new job." I get it. We all have aspirations we're working toward; however, these responses describe the joy of the world, which is based on circumstances, not the joy of the kingdom, which is available in abundance all the time.

It's easy to confuse joy and happiness. Happiness is an emotional response to our external circumstances. If you open a gift on Christmas morning that's exactly what you were hoping for, you'll be happy. Joy, on the other hand, can be present even if there are no presents under the tree and life is difficult. It is a deeper reality that flows from the core of our being.

DAY
14

Put simply, joy is produced by God, not purchased by us.

Every holiday season, marketers unleash an impressive strategy of making us want something we don't have and convincing us we'll be happy if we get it. As Mark Sayers has said, "Once upon a time products were sold on the merit of their function. People were told, 'Buy this bar of soap because it will make you clean'; 'Buy this suit because it is well made'; 'Buy this car because it is safe and will be economical for your family.'"[1] But advertising has moved from function to experience. Now products guarantee joy. "Buy this toothpaste because it will make you happy or joyful." "Buy this car because you will attract women and feel desirable." "Buy these clothes because you will gain status."

Buying things can deliver a momentary thrill, but it soon fades. The kind of joy we desperately need can be produced only by God. That is why Paul named it as a fruit of the Spirit: something that grows organically from a life rooted in God.

Right now, do a quick audit of your habits of spending and consuming: How much money and time do you spend looking for joy in things? I don't pose this question to heap guilt and shame on you. Truthfully, we *all* chase happiness in fleeting ways. The lure of materialism is strong in the modern world. I bring that up as a reminder to draw near to God, who can ultimately satisfy your soul. Since he *is* joy, the path to joy is spending time in his presence. The newest product inevitably grows obsolete; God is always available. Overflowing with endless joy. Delighting in sharing himself with you.

This Advent season, what would it look like to spend more time with him? To experience joy that never runs out?

• DAY
14

REFLECT

PREPARE: Spend two minutes in silence and stillness before God.

PRAYER FOR PRESENCE: Lord Jesus, in this moment, I believe you want to speak to me in a

deep and personal way. May I be attentive to your loving and merciful voice.

SCRIPTURE | JOHN 15:9–12

GUIDE: Joy is always the by-product of something else. . . . We can never attain joy, consolation, peace, forgiveness, love, and understanding by actively pursuing them. . . . Joy will come to us if we set about actively trying to create it for others.[2]

—RONALD ROLHEISER

QUESTION: How have you experienced joy by seeking the Lord? How might you pursue more of his presence in this season?

DAY
14

CLOSING PRAYER: May the Lord bless us and keep us and cause his face to shine upon us from this day forth and forevermore. Amen.

DAY 15

JOY THROUGH SINGING

I was once a worship leader. Not by choice. In the small church I became a Christian at, *everyone* took turns leading in song. Miriam, one of my first mothers in the faith, looked at me one day and said, "Next Sunday, you'll open our service with three songs." As a new Christian, I don't think I *knew* three songs. But seven days later, there I was, microphone in hand in front of a Latino congregation of forty people. Thankfully, ten seconds into the song, the musicians drowned me out with their loud instruments.

I had the privilege of leading the singing a handful of times, and each time, I was struck by the joy it brought me. Now, to be clear, God has not given me the gift of singing. Rosie cringes every time I start off the Happy Birthday song. But that has never stopped me from singing. I sing in the shower. I sing in the car. I sing at the grocery store. I sing while I'm washing dishes. I sing at church. I'm a singer, and I delight in it! (And, yes, I realize that my singing might not be delightful to your ears.)

Singing has been a core part of my faith. I was taught to sing like Paul and Silas (see Acts 16:25) when I found myself in a challenging situation. I was discipled by wise elders to sing because God inhabits the praises of his people. As someone who frequents monasteries annually, I cherish the practice Christian monks have of singing the entire Psalter each month.

The Advent season brings with it the custom of caroling. But spiritually, our lives need more than a short season in a given year to sing. We must cultivate a practice of singing, because it is one of the means by which joy enters our lives.

DAY
15

It may surprise you, but research shows that singing is good for you in a myriad of ways. Here are a few practical benefits:

- Singing lowers cortisol and relieves stress and tension.

- Singing boosts confidence.

- Singing is a mindful activity.

- Singing strengthens the immune system.[1]

As you can see, singing is good for overall health. But there's even more benefit when we sing songs of *praise.* In the book of James, there's a simple verse that says, "Is anyone happy? Let them sing songs of praise" (5:13). That seems obvious: When someone is happy, it's natural to sing. However, it's those last three words—"songs of praise"—that make all the difference.

It's one thing to belt out your favorite pop song (or, in my case, nineties hip-hop) on a road trip; it's another to worship through song, because as we do, we're reminded of God's saving work throughout history. Singing songs of praise helps us connect the *joys* of life to the *source* of life. As your mouth sings, so your soul rejoices.

This Advent, what would it look like to sing songs of praise? To make it a regular part of your day?

REFLECT

PREPARE: Spend two minutes in silence and stillness before God.

PRAYER FOR PRESENCE: Lord Jesus, in this moment of prayer, free me from the distractions of the day so that I may be deeply present to you and myself for the sake of the world around me.

——— SCRIPTURE | JOHN 16:16–24 ———

GUIDE: Joy is the rarest and most infrequent thing in the world. We already have enough fanatical seriousness, enthusiasm, and humorless zeal in the world. But joy? This shows us that the perception of the living God is rare. When we have found God our Savior—or when he has found us—we will rejoice in him.

Joy is the simplest form of gratitude.[2]

—KARL BARTH

QUESTION: Take a few minutes and listen to or sing a worship song that stirs your heart toward joy in the Lord.

CLOSING PRAYER: Our Father in heaven, hallowed be your name, your kingdom come, your will be done, on earth as it is in heaven. Give us today our daily bread. And forgive us our debts, as we also have forgiven our debtors. And lead us not into temptation, but deliver us from the evil one.

DAY
15

FOLLOWING CHILDREN INTO JOY

When I took my daughter, Karis, to the playground for the first time, I put her on the swings. Although her vocabulary was limited, her joy was undeniable. Every time she swung forward, our gazes would meet, and by the delighted look in her eyes, you would have thought I had given her a million dollars.

"Again! Again!" she kept saying.

Maybe you've noticed that the older we get, the more delight-deficient we become. That is why we need the gift and presence of children. Children are carriers of joy because they live in wonder. Every day, there's something new to learn. A fresh source of delight. Their zeal for life is contagious.

The Advent season reminds us that God didn't arrive on

this planet as a fully grown man; he came as a tiny infant. An infant who tasted joy and delight as he aged. An infant who embodied joy as he grew. Even as a man, Jesus invited children to come near, when other adults wouldn't make room for them.

On one occasion, Jesus said, "Let the little children come to me, and do not hinder them, for the kingdom of heaven belongs to such as these" (Matthew 19:14). Another time, Jesus made childlikeness the gateway to entrance into the kingdom of God: "Truly I tell you, unless you change and become like little children, you will never enter the kingdom of heaven" (18:3).

Of all the reasons Jesus referenced little children as the key to entering the kingdom of heaven, I imagine their ability for wonder, amazement, and joy is high on the list. So many adults in Jesus's day—like today—had lost that capacity. God was in their midst, but they couldn't see that. To those with closed eyes and hearts, Jesus says a conversion is needed. When we think of a conversion, we might picture an atheist who decides to follow Christ. But there's another conversion Jesus highlights: adults who become more like children.

In the natural order of human life, we expect children to mature into adulthood. That is good, in a sense. However, in the kingdom of God, Jesus also calls adults to mature into childlikeness (which is quite different from being child*ish*). Children have a maturity that eludes many adults. It's the

DAY
16

95

capacity for joy. This capacity is one of the great expressions of the character of God. G. K. Chesterton captures this idea beautifully:

> Grown-up people are not strong enough to exult in monotony. But perhaps God is strong enough to exult in monotony. It is possible that God says every morning, "Do it again" to the sun; and every evening, "Do it again" to the moon. It may not be automatic necessity that makes all daisies alike; it may be that God makes every daisy separately, but has never got tired of making them. It may be that He has the eternal appetite of infancy; for we have sinned and grown old, and our Father is younger than we.[1]

This Advent, perhaps God is inviting you to become more like a child. Don't let that sting your pride; let it spark your imagination. Wonder is all around you. Do you see it?

REFLECT

PREPARE: Spend two minutes in silence and stillness before God.

PRAYER FOR PRESENCE: Lord Jesus, in this moment, I believe you want to speak to me in a

deep and personal way. May I be attentive to your loving and merciful voice.

——— SCRIPTURE | PHILIPPIANS 4:4–7 ———

GUIDE: The beginning of our happiness lies in the understanding that life without wonder is not worth living. What we lack is not a will to believe but a will to wonder.

Awareness of the divine begins with wonder. . . .

The way to faith leads through acts of wonder and radical amazement.[2]

—Abraham Joshua Heschel

DAY

16

QUESTION: Although the feeling of wonder can't be manufactured or forced, God has wired you to experience it uniquely—perhaps through music, nature, conversation, reading, or singing. What is one simple way you can sit in childlike wonder today?

CLOSING PRAYER: May the Lord bless us and keep us and cause his face to shine upon us from this day forth and forevermore. Amen.

JOY AND SORROW HELD TOGETHER

When most of us think about Christmas, we likely think of things like happiness, laughter, and warmth. However, for many, the holidays are fraught with pain and suffering. That is troubling for me because I don't want to think about suffering when Santa is coming to town. I'd rather watch my favorite movies on rotation in the month of December. You know which movies, right? *Elf. Home Alone. A Christmas Story.* Yeah, the classics. I want to feel cheery and joyous. But this season in the Christian calendar doesn't make it easy on me. And what I've come to realize is that I often settle for superficial emotions during the holidays rather than face the pain of the world—and in my own heart.

The story of the Bible is one of brutal honesty and brokenness. In the world of Holy Scripture, God's people are familiar with both suffering and grief. Rather than choosing between them, they hold them in tension.

In Matthew 2, the birth of Jesus is followed by Herod's ruthless attack on small children. Joy and sorrow intermingle in a span of sixteen verses. It's a reminder that Advent is a time to hold in tension the reality of darkness and the presence of light; the reality of grief and the presence of joy.

The world says, "Blessed are those without any problems." Or "Blessed are the optimists." Not so fast. In Jesus's kingdom, mourning—not merrymaking—brings blessing. How can this be?

To mourn means to carry our grief to God. To lament. To refuse to sugarcoat life. It's authenticity, looking honestly at the brokenness of the world and the brokenness of our lives.

DAY
17

During college, one of my assignments in a spiritual-formation class was to write an eight-page paper on grief and loss. For the first time, I allowed myself to consider the losses I experienced throughout childhood (including various betrayals of trust, as well as losing family members to premature death). As I processed those experiences, my grief felt overwhelming.

Even today, working through past pain is difficult for me, but I have met God while doing so. I can be easily formed by a world that numbs pain and moves quickly to the next thing. But the joy available in Jesus doesn't come by eliminating grief. We can't numb our emotions without deadening everything else. Paradoxically, no grief means no joy. To compartmentalize or ignore one part of our lives affects the whole.

This Advent season, remember that the same Bible that says "Rejoice . . . always" (Philippians 4:4) has a book called Lamentations. The joy of the Lord arrives not in moments absent of pain but, surprisingly, *in* moments of pain. So we grieve. And we rejoice.

REFLECT

PREPARE: Spend two minutes in silence and stillness before God.

PRAYER FOR PRESENCE: Lord Jesus, in this moment, I believe you want to speak to me in a deep and personal way. May I be attentive to your loving and merciful voice.

——— SCRIPTURE | HABAKKUK 3:16–18 ———

GUIDE: Joy is what makes life worth living, but for many joy seems hard to find. They complain that their lives are sorrowful and depressing. What then brings the joy we so much desire? Are some people just lucky, while others have run out of luck? Strange as it may sound, we can choose joy. Two people can be part of the same event, but one may choose to live it quite differently from the other. One may choose to trust that what happened, painful as it may be, holds a promise. The other may choose despair and be destroyed by it.

What makes us human is precisely this freedom of choice.[1]

—Henri Nouwen

QUESTION: What are you grieving right now? What are you rejoicing about right now? How can you hold those two together during this season?

CLOSING PRAYER: May the Lord bless us and keep us and cause his face to shine upon us from this day forth and forevermore. Amen.

DAY
17

JESUS, BRINGER OF JOY

J oy is a central aspect of being a Christian. We know we are called to feel joy and express it, yet it can feel beyond our grasp. But Advent offers a promise. The promise is not just some generic sense of joy; it's the very joy of Jesus. Think about this: Have you ever considered that the joy Jesus carries can be yours? To return to one of my core Scripture texts, in John 15:11, he says to his disciples, "I have told you this so that my joy may be in you and that your joy may be complete."

Christ desires to fill you with his joy. What a thought. In that same chapter, Jesus gives us two ways to open our lives to his happiness: Abide in God and love our neighbor. Let's consider those instructions.

Jesus starts his day by calling his disciples to "abide" in him (see verse 4, ESV). There are more than sixty instances of the word *abide* in John's writings, so it's an important word. To live with Jesus's joy, we must linger with him. Continually turn back to him. Be with him.

It's no accident that multiple times Jesus tells his disciples to abide. He knows we tend to drift away. On any given day, we get distracted and busy. I often find myself irritable and anxious. In those moments, Jesus calls me to abide in him. Advent is the annual reminder that true joy doesn't come because gifts are under the tree or because Mariah Carey's "All I Want for Christmas Is You" is playing on the sound system; it comes because we are returning to Jesus repeatedly.

Beyond abiding in him, Jesus gives us a second way to receive his joy: through loving others. Right after he shares his desire to make our joy complete, he commands us, "Love each other as I have loved you" (verse 12). The source of his happiness was his love for others. That is how joy works in the kingdom of God: The quality of our joy is directly connected to the quality of our love.

DAY
18

For Jesus, joy is not oriented around personal feelings of happiness that stem from a positive outlook on life. Joy is deeply relational. I can't help but think that Jesus's joy was off the charts because he lived in service to others. In Jesus, God became a human in order to pour out his life for the sake of the well-being of others. One of the secrets to a joy-saturated life is that we're surprised when joy is not our focus. Our attempts to live with joy get compromised when our feelings are the primary drivers of our decisions. That is why there is great danger during Advent. We are made to believe that consuming more will make us joyful. We are discipled by our world to entrust our joy to the next big purchase. But Jesus's joy cannot be bought. It is secured as we serve. It is received as we love.

REFLECT

PREPARE: Spend two minutes in silence and stillness before God.

PRAYER FOR PRESENCE: Lord Jesus, in this moment, I believe you want to speak to me in a deep and personal way. May I be attentive to your loving and merciful voice.

DAY
18

SCRIPTURE | JOHN 17:6–13

GUIDE: Joy is a deep-seated sense of well-being, of safety in God's universe. Joy is part of the fruit of the Spirit, growing as a natural product of the transformation of one's inner self to be like that of Christ, which itself is full of joy. We should, to begin with, think that God leads a very interesting life, and that he is full of joy. Undoubtedly, he is the most joyous being in the universe. The abundance of his love and generosity is inseparable from his infinite joy. All of the good and beautiful things from which we occasionally drink tiny droplets of soul exhilarating joy, God continuously experiences in all their breadth and depth and richness.[1]

—DALLAS WILLARD

QUESTION: Think about Jesus's commands to abide in him and to love others. How can you obey those commands this week? As you do, pay attention to the joy you experience along the way.

CLOSING PRAYER: May the Lord bless us and keep us and cause his face to shine upon us from this day forth and forevermore. Amen.

DAY

18

PART FOUR

BEHOLDING

BEHOLDING GOD

With Christianity, it's easy to focus on believing and behaving, but what often goes overlooked is the spiritual habit of beholding. To behold God is an act of patient attentiveness. It's a way to remind our hearts of the remarkable news that he has drawn near to us. It's transformative, because we become what we behold.

Theologian Maggie Ross has suggested that *behold* might be the most important word in the Bible. When that word shows up, there's a point to be made. Just look at the following Scripture passages.[1]

> Behold! He is coming with the clouds and everyone shall see him. (Revelation 1:7)

Behold! The hour comes. (John 16:32)

Behold! I bring you good tidings. (Luke 2:10)

Behold! The Lion of Judah. (Revelation 5:5)

Behold! I am laying in Zion a foundation stone. (Isaiah 28:16)

Behold! I am sending a messenger. (Malachi 3:1)

Behold! The bridegroom comes. (Matthew 25:6)

DAY
19

Behold! I tell you a mystery. (1 Corinthians 15:51)

Behold! The Lamb of God. (John 1:36)

We were made to behold—to gaze in wonder at the Creator—but the story of our lives is that we behold many other things. We get distracted. In our state of sin, we fix our hearts and attention on things that block attentiveness to God.

Yet the gospel reminds us that God always has his eye on us. From Genesis to Revelation, we discover a God who is lovingly present with his people. That is the good news of Advent.

So, how can we behold God?

- To behold God is to fix our eyes on Jesus in the Gospels.

- To behold God is to find ourselves in the stories of the Bible, recognizing that anyone who came to Jesus for help is a representation of us. Whether we are blind, hungry, lonely, or crushed by injustice, when we see it and turn to Jesus, we open ourselves to his presence.

- To behold God is to practice stillness on an ordinary day. It's pausing to remember that every breath we take comes from him.

DAY
19

- To behold God is to lift our minds and hearts to God in prayer.

- To behold God is to meditate on Holy Scripture, allowing the truth of God's Word to penetrate our lives.

Advent is an appeal to our attention. Will we choose to behold God or distract ourselves to get through another day? What has your attention this holiday season? What have you been beholding? I pray that you glimpse more of God's glory and goodness this season. He is with you, and he is worth adoring.

REFLECT

PREPARE: Spend two minutes in silence and stillness before God.

PRAYER FOR PRESENCE: Lord Jesus, in this moment, I believe you want to speak to me in a deep and personal way. May I be attentive to your loving and merciful voice.

———— SCRIPTURE | JOHN 1:29-34 ————

GUIDE: *Behold.* Behold the God who is infinitely more humble than those who pray to him, more stripped, more emptied, more self-outpouring—and we need to remember that humility and humiliation are mutually exclusive. Humility knows only love, and God is love. The scandal of the incarnation is not that we are naked before Emmanuel, God with us, but God is naked before us, and, in utter silence, given over into our hands and hearts. And it is in the depths of this beholding, in the silence of the loving heart of God, that the divine exchange takes place most fully, where each of us in our uniqueness and strangeness is transfigured into the divine life. And it is for this that God comes to us, the Word made flesh, stable-born and crucified.[2]

—MAGGIE ROSS

112

QUESTION: How can you set apart time to behold God today? What is a distraction you need to eliminate?

CLOSING PRAYER: May the Lord bless us and keep us and cause his face to shine upon us from this day forth and forevermore. Amen.

DAY
19

SAYING YES TO
GOD'S INVITATIONS

as God ever interrupted your plans? Perhaps it was through meeting someone who changed your life, an unplanned career shift or layoff, or an opportunity you didn't see coming. For Mary, the mother of Jesus, all her plans changed the day God sent an angel to visit her. She was a young woman engaged to be married. In modern terms, she was the person who created a website for her wedding. She set up a gift registry at her favorite store. She sent out the invitations to friends and family. Amid the planning and dreaming, there's one invitation Mary never expected to get.

As she was alone one day, thinking about her future husband and family, God interrupted her plans. An angel named Gabriel approached her, announcing the most unimaginable news: She would give birth to the Savior of the world (see Luke 1:26–38). I assure you that was not what she thought she would hear when she woke up. So much must have been swirling in her head. She'd be risking her reputation to say yes to that invitation. Each year, three-quarters of a million teenage girls in the United States get pregnant out of wedlock, so it can be easy for us to miss the scandal of this event. In biblical times, to get pregnant before marriage made a woman an adulteress, subject to death by stoning.

Mary asked the angel how she would get pregnant, and Gabriel responded with the famous line "The Holy Spirit will come on you, and the power of the Most High will overshadow you" (verse 35). Recognizing that God was doing something unprecedented, Mary said, "Let it be" (verse 38, ESV). No part of her felt prepared, but she was willing. That is the message of Advent. Responding to God's invitations doesn't require us to be ready; we just have to be willing.

DAY 20

In his book *Sacred Fire,* Ron Rolheiser wrote,

Not even Jesus found "the ready."
Jesus called Nathaniel . . . Nathaniel lacked
   openness. Nathaniel wasn't ready.
Jesus called Philip . . . Philip lacked simplicity.
   Philip wasn't ready.
Jesus called Simon, the Zealot . . . Simon lacked
   non-violence. Simon wasn't ready.
Jesus called Andrew . . . Andrew lacked a sense of
   risk. Andrew wasn't ready.
Jesus called Thomas . . . Thomas lacked vision.
   Thomas wasn't ready.

> Jesus called Judas . . . Judas lacked spiritual
> maturity. Judas was definitely not ready.
> Jesus called Matthew . . . Matthew lacked a sense
> of social sin. Matthew wasn't ready.
> Jesus called Thaddeus . . . Thaddeus lacked
> commitment. Thaddeus wasn't ready.
> Jesus called James the Lesser . . . James lacked
> awareness. James wasn't ready.
> Jesus called James and John, the sons of
> thunder . . . James and John lacked a sense of
> servanthood. James and John were not ready.
> Jesus called Peter, the Rock . . . Peter lacked
> courage. Peter was not ready. . . .
> The point, you see, is that Jesus doesn't call the
> ready. Jesus calls the willing.[1]

While none of us will receive Mary's call to give birth to Jesus, we all have an invitation from God to help renew the world. In big and small ways, we can partner with him to bring light into it. What does it look like to say yes to this invitation?

REFLECT

PREPARE: Spend two minutes in silence and stillness before God.

PRAYER FOR PRESENCE: Lord Jesus, in this moment, I believe you want to speak to me in a

deep and personal way. May I be attentive to your loving and merciful voice.

———— SCRIPTURE | LUKE 1:26–38 ————

GUIDE: You have loved us first, O God, alas! We speak of it in terms of history as if You loved us first but a single time, . . . [but] You have loved us first many times and everyday and our whole life through. When we wake up in the morning and turn our soul toward You—You are there first—You have loved us first; if I rise at dawn and at that same second turn my soul toward You in prayer, You are there ahead of me, You have loved me first. When I withdraw from the distractions of the day and turn my soul toward You, You are there first and thus forever. And we speak ungratefully as if You have loved us first only once.[2]

—Søren Kierkegaard

QUESTION: What is something you sense God inviting you to do, think, or say? How can you position your heart to say yes to him?

CLOSING PRAYER: May the Lord bless us and keep us and cause his face to shine upon us from this day forth and forevermore. Amen.

SLOWING DOWN TO PONDER

Driving in New York City is far more expensive than it used to be. In the not-too-distant past, if you were speeding, a police officer would catch you in the act, pull you over, and place a ticket in your hand. Nowadays, there's a far more efficient way to curb speedsters. In various parts of the city, cameras have been set up. If you're going beyond the limit, you'll get a nice bill in the mail. Over the years, I've gone to the mailbox only to discover a fine I had to pay. Speed is costly.

Our rapid pace of living also affects us spiritually. A fast-paced life creates a worn-down soul. To ponder God's Word, to let it sink deep, we must pause. Linger to hear his voice. Slow down to savor his love. That is why Advent season is a gift: It reminds us to reflect on God's gracious acts toward us.

That is what we see in Mary, the mother of Jesus. After the hosts of heaven praised God because of the Messiah's arrival, Mary "treasured up all these things and pondered them in her heart" (Luke 2:19). Rather than going through the motions or getting distracted by the immensity of what was happening, she took time to reflect. She stepped back, noting all God was doing.

When I think about Mary's capacity to ponder, I'm inspired and convicted. Advent tells of a God who is at work in the world. At this very moment, he is moving toward us in love. We might not see angels singing, but the presence of God is near. (As I write these words, I'm at a park, overhearing the laughter and squealing of small children playing with one another. Surely, God is here.)

DAY
21

Perhaps, like me, you are prone to distraction and busyness. You find it difficult to slow down and contemplate. You feel constantly hurried, desperately scrambling to complete an endless list of to-dos. It could be that you stay busy to numb your emotions because you're afraid to face yourself. Maybe you're tempted to build your identity based on accomplishments. Regardless, Jesus invites you to slow down and contemplate.

Please receive this Advent truth: It is possible to live a life in which you are present to God, yourself, and others. A life not dictated by hurry, rushing, and speed. You were created to ponder. To treasure the words of God in your heart. The choice to slow down, to reflect, will give vitality to your soul.

Mary pondered. So can you.

REFLECT

PREPARE: Spend two minutes in silence and stillness before God.

PRAYER FOR PRESENCE: Lord Jesus, in this moment, I believe you want to speak to me in a deep and personal way. May I be attentive to your loving and merciful voice.

——— SCRIPTURE | PSALM 111 ———

GUIDE: The way of Jesus cannot be imposed or mapped—it requires an active participation in following Jesus as he leads us through sometimes strange and unfamiliar territory, in circumstances that become clear only in the hesitations and questionings, in the pauses and reflections where we engage in prayerful conversation with one another and with him.[1]

—Eugene Peterson

QUESTION: What is one thing God has done in your life that you'd like to ponder? Spend a few moments, right now, processing with him what happened.

CLOSING PRAYER: May the Lord bless us and keep us and cause his face to shine upon us from this day forth and forevermore. Amen.

BEHOLDING THE "GOD WITH US"

ong before Jesus was born, the prophet Isaiah saw a day when a virgin would conceive and give birth to a son. His name would be *Emmanuel*. This Hebrew name would be translated into three English words: "God with us." They are the three most important words of Advent and Christmas.

It's quite easy to gloss over them, because we are familiar with the story. But Isaiah saw something that we need to take our time with. So let's explore each word briefly.

GOD

This is the first word of Christmas: *God*! At Christmastime, we don't say a great prophet has come (although that is true). We don't say a marvelous teacher has come (true as well). We don't say a great man has come (also true). Instead, we dare to say *God* has come. It's an audacious claim. And if it's true, it changes everything. Whenever I really give thought to that, it messes with my brain. *God* has come to earth. All of history hinges on that event. Our lives can be understood only in light of it.

What makes this event even more scandalous is *how* God came: not as a domineering ruler or wealthy king but as a vulnerable baby. Babies are known for four things: crying, eating, sleeping, and pooping. Not impressive. Advent reminds us that billions of galaxies, the highest mountain, and the deepest sea were all created through this child.

DAY

22

WITH

Here we have the best news in the world: God doesn't merely exist; he draws near. He takes on human flesh because he wants to be *with* us. Sometimes it's easier to picture a God who is *against* us.

Maybe life hasn't unfolded the way we wanted it to. Maybe we are filled with disappointment. Maybe we've experienced crisis and setback and pain and concluded that God is not on our side. Perhaps people around us seem to enjoy success, while *we* struggle. Christmas can be a depressing season: a time to avoid God because we somehow suspect we've let him down and now he's angry with us.

Or rather than God *with* us, we imagine a God who is *apart* from us. A God who seems disconnected, distant, and disinterested in our lives. Perhaps we feel spiritually lonely, unsure how to connect with God and his people. A gnawing sense of isolation is one of the most potent problems of our day. However, Matthew (the gospel writer) reminds us that whether we feel it or not, whether we believe it or not, God is with us. Which brings us to the final word.

US

To say it yet again, God wants to be with us. When you understand who *us* is, it makes the other two words that much more powerful. If we were righteous, sinless, perfect people, you would think, yes, of course God wants to be with us. But the surprise of Christmas is that he wants to be with broken, sinful, irritable, cursing, rebellious us. The *real* us, rough edges and all. That is grace.

Whether you've been a Christian for twenty years or exploring faith for two weeks, God wants to be with you. If it sounds too good to be true, grace always does. Draw near to him this Advent.

DAY
22

REFLECT

PREPARE: Spend two minutes in silence and stillness before God.

PRAYER FOR PRESENCE: Lord Jesus, in this moment, I believe you want to speak to me in a

deep and personal way. May I be attentive to your loving and merciful voice.

GUIDE: The incarnate God is called *Emmanuel,* a name which means *God-is-with-us.* That fact does not mean immediate festive joy. . . . Pain lingers. . . .

The incarnation does not promise us heaven on earth. It promises heaven in heaven. Here, on earth, it promises us something else—*God's presence in our lives.*"[1]

—RON ROLHEISER

DAY
22

QUESTION: Reflect on the wonderful reality that God wants to be with you. If you really believed that, how would it change your life?

CLOSING PRAYER: May the Lord bless us and keep us and cause his face to shine upon us from this day forth and forevermore. Amen.

HOLY SILENCE AND SOLITUDE

Solitude and silence have shaped my spiritual journey since my early twenties. Soon after making a decision to follow Jesus, I carried many questions about the next steps to take in my newfound faith. Thankfully, I had to take only a few steps down the block to my grandfather's Brooklyn home. That man, Marcos Rios, was a contemplative. At seventy-seven years of age, he had walked with Christ for decades, prioritizing a regular practice of solitude and reflection.

A few days after coming to faith in Christ, I went into his tight-quartered bedroom flanked with antique furniture and a window fan to cool him on that hot summer evening. He had the Bible on his lap and a jar of M&M'S on his nightstand. At every page turn, he'd pop one of the candies into his mouth.

I sheepishly entered his presence with a question about the Bible. He invited me to sit next to him, offered me some M&M'S, and opened my eyes to the scriptures. Over the next eight months, four or five days a week, two to three hours each session, we talked about faith. There were many great theological lessons over that period, but what I remember most was his contemplative way of being. He made lots of room for silence and solitude.

His bedroom was my first monastery. It's where I first learned to behold God.

Depending on whom you talk to, the words *silence* and *solitude* are either good words or hard words. How do *you* think of them?

Whether you're enthusiastic or hesitant about them, silence and solitude are indispensable practices for growing in spiritual maturity. At their core, they create space to connect with God. They convert our aloneness into attentiveness. Solitude isn't simply about creating distance from others; it's about paying close attention to ourselves and, most important, God.

In Scripture, when Elizabeth received news that she would bear a son (John the Baptist), she entered a season of solitude. After years of infertility, she was advanced in age. But God graciously answered her prayer to become pregnant, and for five months, she found a secluded place (see Luke 1:24). There are many reasons for this, but I believe that like Mary, she needed space to focus on what God was doing in her life.

That is what solitude and silence offer us. The Advent season can feel very crowded. There's lots to do. Homes to prepare. Gifts to purchase. Food to cook. But like Elizabeth, we can all benefit from silence and solitude. By pursuing those disciplines, we will have space to center ourselves in a time when we are pulled in many directions. To be with God and enjoy his presence.

REFLECT

PREPARE: Spend two minutes in silence and stillness before God.

PRAYER FOR PRESENCE: Lord Jesus, in this moment, I believe you want to speak to me in a deep and personal way. May I be attentive to your loving and merciful voice.

DAY

23

—— SCRIPTURE | LUKE 1:5–25 ——

GUIDE: Silence can be a dreadful ordeal with all its desolation and terrors. It can also be a false paradise of self-deception; the latter is no better than the former. Be that as it may, let none expect from silence anything but a direct encounter with the Word of God, for the sake of which he has entered into silence. But this encounter will be given to him. The Christian will not lay down any conditions as to what he expects or hopes to get from this encounter. If he will simply accept it, his silence will be richly rewarded.[1]

—DIETRICH BONHOEFFER

QUESTION: In this busy season, how can you carve out more time for silence and solitude? Even if it's five minutes once a week, when and where can you seek God's presence outside life's noise?

CLOSING PRAYER: May the Lord bless us and keep us and cause his face to shine upon us from this day forth and forevermore. Amen.

DAY
23

BEHOLDING OUR BROKENNESS

Although Advent is a season of great joy, it loses its significance when it's disconnected from the fundamental need of humanity: rescue from our sin and brokenness. The degree to which we recognize our need for God's rescue is the degree to which we will become the people we're created to be.

Over the years, I've heard people say that religion in general (and Christianity in particular) is for weak people: those who need a crutch to help them get through life. I remember having a conversation with someone who mentioned this need for religion's "crutch." I told him I disagreed with his portrayal of Christianity. As he prepared to state his case, I told him that Christianity was more than a crutch for the weak; it's a wheelchair. A gurney. A hospital. Better yet, it's a hearse.

Christianity doesn't correct a minor limp; it announces that we are dead and in need of a power outside ourselves to bring us to life. That's why when Joseph is told by an angel that the child in Mary's womb is the Messiah, this description is given: "He will save his people from their sins" (Matthew 1:21). Sin and brokenness mark our world. To truly appreciate what Jesus has done, we must recognize the severity of the problem.

My friend Glenn Packiam has described sin in a few helpful ways:

DAY
24

> There are (at least) three dimensions of "sin" that I see in the New Testament:
>
> 1. Sin is a CONDITION (a Power we are under that keeps us enslaved)
> 2. Sin is a CONTAGION (an infection that inhibits our capacity and spread[s] easily)
> 3. Sin is a DECISION (a choice we have moral culpability in)
>
> Without understanding 1 and 2, we are likely to overplay guilt and shame, preventing people from longing for freedom and healing. Without acknowledging 3, we are quick to blame environmental or situational factors for our actions and behaviors.
>
> But when we see all three layers, we can stand in awe of the salvation that Jesus brings:

Jesus FREES us from the power of sin.
Jesus HEALS us from the infection of sin.
Jesus FORGIVES us from the guilt of sin.[1]

Because of sin, our brokenness runs deep. But because of Jesus, healing runs deeper.

During this Advent, call upon the name of the Lord. The world is under the power of sin, but a day is coming when the world will be under the power of love. The world is infected with all kinds of illness, but a day is coming when healing will pervade all creation. Our hearts are often plagued by guilt and shame, but one day we will live in the fullness of grace.

So we look to the one who will save us from our sin.

DAY
24

REFLECT

PREPARE: Spend two minutes in silence and stillness before God.

PRAYER FOR PRESENCE: Lord Jesus, in this moment, I believe you want to speak to me in a deep and personal way. May I be attentive to your loving and merciful voice.

——— SCRIPTURE | MATTHEW 1:18–21 ———

GUIDE: God entered into our world not with the crushing impact of unbearable glory, but in the way of weakness, vulnerability, and need. The world does not understand vulnerability. Neediness is rejected as incompetence, and compassion is dismissed as unprofitable. But in this weakness and poverty the shipwrecked at the stable would come to know the love of God.[2]

—BRENNAN MANNING

QUESTION: In regard to the three aspects of sin—condition, contagion, decision—which do you feel most strongly? Take a few moments and process this with God.

CLOSING PRAYER: May the Lord bless us and keep us and cause his face to shine upon us from this day forth and forevermore. Amen.

THE KING IS BORN (CHRISTMAS DAY)

There were shepherds living out in the fields nearby, keeping watch over their flocks at night. An angel of the Lord appeared to them, and the glory of the Lord shone around them, and they were terrified. But the angel said to them, "Do not be afraid. I bring you good news that will cause great joy for all the people. Today in the town of David a Savior has been born to you; he is the Messiah, the Lord. This will be a sign to you: You will find a baby wrapped in cloths and lying in a manger."

—LUKE 2:8–12

Not too long ago, I was on an airplane and as the plane was taking off, there was a little boy not too far from my seat. The little boy was squealing with joy and wonder, so much so that I had to look out the window to see if he saw something I didn't. And the truth is that he did. He saw the wonder of the moment.

Over a year ago, I made my first trip to Colorado, and as I was driving, I saw the majestic and powerful mountains in the distance. I asked someone who's lived there for a long time, "Do you ever get tired of that view?"

He said, "Well, sometimes I don't even pay attention to it."

Familiarity breeds apathy. We can be so comfortable with things that we miss the wonder of it all. Similarly, the Christmas story is one that we can easily gloss over, even when it's right in front of us. Sure, we know the story. That's not the issue. The question is, are we *gripped* by it?

The story begins with an angel sent by God to deliver good news. In the simple words "An angel of the Lord appeared to them" (Luke 2:9), the heart of God is demonstrated to us. It's a reminder that it's always *God* who comes to us first, not the other way around. He's the one who takes the initiative, runs to greet prodigals, and seeks out lost sheep. Be reminded this Christmas that before you sought God, he found you.

When the angel announces this good news about God seeking his people, the message is "Unto you is born this day . . . a Savior" (verse 11, ESV). Let's unpack this short but powerful statement.

DAY
25

UNTO YOU

When our children were little, Christmastime was always a funny thing. As the big day approached, our son, Nathan (who was three at the time), would say every ten minutes or so, "I'm behaving, right, Daddy?" Somehow he understood morality and ethics and the fruit of the Spirit when Christmas got close.

Another thing he'd ask was, "What's Santa Claus doing now? Is he making presents?"

"Yes," I'd say, "and he's delivering them to everyone in the world."

"Yeah, but is he going to bring some to me?"

"Yes, son. Everyone in the whole world."

"But is he going to bring it to *me*?"

On the surface, Nathan—like most kids—was simply concerned about his chances of receiving presents that year. However, dig a little deeper and you'll see he was expressing the inner fear we all have about God. We know in our heads he loves us, but sometimes our hearts aren't so sure. We wonder, *Is God really for* me?

DAY
25

Notice what the angel *doesn't* say: Unto you (who have been good). Unto you (who have been saying your prayers). Unto you (who have been sexually pure). Unto you (who deserve it). None of that! All we hear the angel say is "Unto you"! It's God's way of saying that regardless of who you are, regardless of what you've done (or haven't done), he has come for you.

Christ's birth, while it's good news for the world, is also meant for your individual heart. Christmas is for you, my friend. God has a message with your name on it.

IS BORN

When a baby is born, it's truly a miracle. A divine mystery. Yet it's commonplace. Every day, almost ten thousand babies are born in the United States.[1] That's close to *four million* children annually. Two thousand years ago, when Jesus was born, on one level it was just like any other birth, but from another angle, it was categorically different. Jesus was not just a baby; he was God.

Think about that for a second. We've become so familiar with those words that they no longer shock us. The fact that God "is born" is the greatest mystery and paradox of the Christian faith:

- The defender of the weak becomes small and defenseless.

- The one who covers all becomes naked and exposed.

- The one who cares for all becomes helpless and needy.

- The one who holds it all together shivers in the night and needs to be held tightly.

When we gaze into the eyes of this baby, we're looking into the face of almighty God.

THIS DAY

When the angels say, "This day," they're referring to more than a single day in history; they're announcing that a new era has come. It's here now. This story isn't merely a tale from two thousand years ago; it's a statement about the world we live in and how to make sense of it.

It's a story that's still unfolding. And you're part of it.

Notice the angel shows up at night, yet basically says, "On *this day* a Savior is born." Christ's arrival signaled the dawning of a new day. The end of darkness. Take in this truth: Even when the darkness feels overwhelming, the light of Christ shines bright on the horizon, promising a glorious day when . . .

DAY
25

- trouble and pain and sin will forever be silenced

- you will see him face-to-face

- you will no longer struggle with doubt, insecurity, or trauma

- evil will be dethroned and Christ will reign in his glory

- past wounds will be forever healed

- the world we long for will become reality

If today these promises feel far-fetched or out of reach, remind yourself that in Christ, a light has dawned. Don't give up: The morning is coming.

A SAVIOR

The Christmas story is one of salvation. To say that God has been born is not enough. The God who comes is the God who saves. He showed up not to condemn but to rescue. To break off the shackles of sin.

When I lived in an apartment in Queens, I saw a sign in the lobby that mentioned a recent series of burglaries in the neighborhood. It instructed residents to lock their windows, especially by the fire escape, to keep burglars out. The sign was saying, in effect, "Do all you can to make sure invaders can't come in." It was a helpful reminder.

Without realizing it, many people eye God suspiciously, as though he's a burglar who wants to ruin their joy by heaping religious rules onto their shoulders. Advent reminds us that God *does* want to take things from you but never your joy. He wants to remove things like pride, fear, anxiety, guilt, and shame. His invasions are acts of great love. He breaks in not to rob you but to rescue you.

What glorious news, that God longs to be with us. That his arrival sparked the dawning of a new era—one that's good news for the world.

Unto you. Is born. This day. A Savior.

Merry Christmas!

NOTES

DAY 1—THE FOUNDATION OF THE SPIRITUAL LIFE

1. Simone Weil, quoted in Henri J. M. Nouwen, *Out of Solitude: Three Meditations on the Christian Life* (Ave Maria Press, 2004), 55.
2. Henri J. M. Nouwen, *Eternal Seasons: A Spiritual Journey Through the Church's Year,* ed. Michael Ford (Ave Maria Press, 2007), 38.
3. This closing prayer and the others like it are paraphrased from Numbers 6:24–26.

DAY 2—GOD WORKS IN THE DARK

1. Langston Hughes, *The Collected Poems of Langston Hughes,* ed. Arnold Rampersad (Vintage, 1995), 135. Used by permission.
2. Barbara Brown Taylor, *The Preaching Life: Living Out Your Vocation* (Rowman and Littlefield, 1993), 90–91.
3. Barbara Brown Taylor, *Gospel Medicine* (Rowman and Littlefield, 1995), 153.

DAY 3—REFUSING TO ACT BEFORE GOD ACTS

1. Eugene Peterson (@PetersonDaily), "Waiting in prayer is a disciplined refusal to act before God acts," Twitter, January 4, 2016, 7:12 P.M., https://x.com/PetersonDaily/status/6841956424749 05601.
2. Dietrich Bonhoeffer, *God Is in the Manger: Reflections on Advent and Christmas,* ed. Jana Riess, trans. O. C. Dean, Jr. (Westminster John Knox, 2010), 4.
3. This closing prayer and the others like it are quoted from Matthew 6:9–13.

DAY 4—WAIT TRAINING

1. James A. Kowalski, "Advent: A Four-Week Course on Patience," *The Huffington Post,* May 25, 2011, www.huffingtonpost.com/rev-dr -james-a-kowalski/advent-a-fourweek-course-_b_791744.html.

DAY 5—WAITING FOR THE CHILD

1. Thomas Merton, *Raids on the Unspeakable* (Burns and Oates, 1988), 72–73.

DAY 6—THE FOOLISHNESS OF WAITING

1. Henri J. M. Nouwen, *Bread for the Journey: A Daybook of Wisdom and Faith* (HarperCollins, 2006), 20.

2. Joan Chittister, *The Liturgical Year: The Spiraling Adventure of the Spiritual Life,* The Ancient Practices Series (Thomas Nelson, 2009), 60, 61–62.

DAY 7—JESUS OR HEROD

1. Stanley Hauerwas, in "Recapturing Advent," The Work of the People: Films for Discovery and Transformation, video, 4:18, www .theworkofthepeople.com/recapturing-advent?fbclid=IwAR0VcRDI bazV7ZBnvdF_dwMnzMWLrka9VNp-RBto_xY2dshCRid2JZ pjog0.

DAY 8—SHALOMING THE WORLD

1. Thomas à Kempis, *The Imitation of Christ* (Indo-European Publishing, 2018), bk. 2, chap. 3.

DAY 9—DISRUPTING FALSE PEACE

1. Rich Villodas, *The Narrow Path: How the Subversive Way of Jesus Satisfies Our Souls* (WaterBrook, 2024), 29–30.

2. Dietrich Bonhoeffer, *The Cost of Discipleship* (Simon and Schuster, 1995), 112–13.

DAY 10—PEACE BEYOND UNDERSTANDING

1. See David Edelstein, "An Unforgettable 208-Second Flight Creates a Bureaucratic Frenzy in 'Sully,' " NPR, September 9, 2016, www .npr.org/2016/09/09/493150297/in-sully-a-pilots-heroic-water -landing-and-its-real-life-fallout.

2. Chesley Sullenberger, quoted in Liz Robbins, "Air Traffic Controller

Tells Gripping Tale of Hudson Landing," *The New York Times,* February 24, 2009, www.nytimes.com/2009/02/25/nyregion/25crash.html.

3. John Main, *Word into Silence: A Manual for Christian Meditation* (Canterbury Press Norwich, 2006), 2.

DAY 11—GLORY TO GOD, PEACE TO US

1. "The Westminster Shorter Catechism," Puritan Reformed Theological Seminary, https://prts.edu/wp-content/uploads/2016/12/Shorter_Catechism.pdf, 1.

2. See "Social Media 'Likes' Impact Teens' Brains and Behavior," Association for Psychological Science, May 31, 2016, www.psychologicalscience.org/news/releases/social-media-likes-impact-teens-brains-and-behavior.html.

3. Henri Nouwen, *Seeds of Hope: A Henri Nouwen Reader,* ed. Robert Durback (Doubleday, 1997), 265.

DAY 12—RECEIVING PEACE

1. Paul Froese and Christopher Bader, *America's Four Gods: What We Say About God—and What That Says About Us* (Oxford Press, 2010), 24.

2. Timothy Keller, *The Reason for God: Belief in an Age of Skepticism* (Penguin Random House, 2018), 186.

3. Dallas Willard, *The Divine Conspiracy: Rediscovering Our Hidden Life in God* (HarperCollins, 1998), 212.

DAY 13—INCREASING YOUR JOY

1. Eugene H. Peterson, *A Long Obedience in the Same Direction: Discipleship in an Instant Society* (InterVarsity, 2000), 96–97.

DAY 14—COMPLETE JOY

1. Mark Sayers, *The Trouble with Paris: Following Jesus in a World of Plastic Promises* (Thomas Nelson, 2008), 18.

2. Ron Rolheiser, "A Meditation on Joy," RonRolheiser.com, December 15, 2002, ronrolheiser.com/a-meditation-on-joy/#.W9oFTxNKgWo.

DAY 15—JOY THROUGH SINGING

1. "Why Singing for Health and Wellbeing?," Sing Up Foundation, www.singupfoundation.org/singing-health.

NOTES

2. The first paragraph is from Karl Barth, *Insights: Karl Barth's Reflections on the Life of Faith,* ed. Eberhard Busch, trans. O. C. Dean, Jr. (Westminster John Knox, 2009), 13. The second paragraph is also widely attributed to Karl Barth.

DAY 16—FOLLOWING CHILDREN INTO JOY

1. G. K. Chesterton, *Orthodoxy* (Moody, 2009), 91–92.
2. Abraham Joshua Heschel, *Essential Writings* (Orbis, 2022), 51–52.

DAY 17—JOY AND SORROW HELD TOGETHER

1. Henri J. M. Nouwen, *Bread for the Journey: A Daybook of Wisdom and Faith* (HarperCollins, 2006), 37.

DAY 18—JESUS, BRINGER OF JOY

1. Dallas Willard, *The Divine Conspiracy: Rediscovering Our Hidden Life in God* (HarperCollins, 1998), 62.

DAY 19—BEHOLDING GOD

1. These scriptures are all slightly paraphrased from the English Standard Version except for Matthew 25:6, which is from the King James Version.
2. Maggie Ross, *Writing the Icon of the Heart: In Silence Beholding* (Wipf and Stock, 2013), 11.

DAY 20—SAYING YES TO GOD'S INVITATIONS

1. Ron Rolheiser, *Sacred Fire: A Vision for a Deeper Human and Christian Maturity* (Penguin Random House, 2014), 61.
2. Søren Kierkegaard, quoted in James Bryan Smith, *Embracing the Love of God: The Path and Promise of Christian Life* (HarperCollins, 2008), 13.

DAY 21—SLOWING DOWN TO PONDER

1. Eugene H. Peterson, *The Jesus Way: A Conversation on the Ways That Jesus Is the Way* (Eerdmans, 2011), 18.

DAY 22—BEHOLDING THE "GOD WITH US"

1. Ron Rolheiser, "Incarnation—God Is with Us," RonRolheiser.com, December 19, 2016, https://ronrolheiser.com/incarnation-god-is -with-us.

DAY 23—HOLY SILENCE AND SOLITUDE

1. Dietrich Bonhoeffer, *The Classic Exploration of Christian in Community* (HarperCollins, 2009), 80–81.

DAY 24—BEHOLDING OUR BROKENNESS

1. Glenn Packiam (@gpackiam), "There are (at least) three dimensions of 'sin' that I see in the New Testament," X, November 1, 2024, 9:11 A.M., https://x.com/gpackiam/status/1852367940450148560.

2. Brennan Manning, *A Glimpse of Jesus: The Stranger to Self-Hatred* (HarperCollins, 2010), 138.

DAY 25—THE KING IS BORN (CHRISTMAS DAY)

1. US Birth Certificates Team, "How Many People Are Born a Day in the U.S.?," US Birth Certificates, January 29, 2025, www.usbirth certificates.com/articles/people-born-daily.

ABOUT THE AUTHOR

RICH VILLODAS is the Brooklyn-born lead pastor of New Life Fellowship, a large multiracial church with more than seventy-five countries represented, in Elmhurst, Queens. Villodas is the author of several books, including the award-winning *Deeply Formed Life,* plus *Good and Beautiful and Kind* and *The Narrow Path.* He and his wife, Rosie, have two beautiful children and reside in New York. Follow Rich on social media with @richvillodas.

ABOUT THE TYPE

This book was set in Garamond, a typeface originally designed by the Parisian type cutter Claude Garamond (c. 1500–61). This version of Garamond was modeled on a 1592 specimen sheet from the Egenolff-Berner foundry, which was produced from types assumed to have been brought to Frankfurt by the punch cutter Jacques Sabon (c. 1520–80).

Claude Garamond's distinguished romans and italics first appeared in Opera Ciceronis in 1543–44. The Garamond types are clear, open, and elegant.

Also from bestselling author
RICH VILLODAS

Be reintroduced to the counterintuitive wonder of Jesus's timeless teachings about the broad and narrow paths—and how they are relevant to our lives today.

Filled with fresh energy, classic truth, and practical solutions, this book is your road map for stepping beyond distraction and division to love like Jesus.

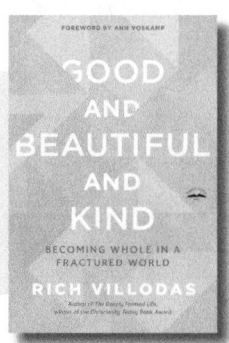

Discover five transformative values to root us in the way of Jesus: a place of communion with God and where we find our purpose amid chaotic times.

Learn more about Rich's books at waterbrookmultnomah.com.

01 14

✓